To:

_____

From:

_____

Date:

_____

The
Jesus
Answer Book

JOHN MACARTHUR

THOMAS NELSON
Since 1798

NASHVILLE   MEXICO CITY   RIO DE JANEIRO

Published in Nashville, Tennessee, by Thomas Nelson. Thomas Nelson is a registered trademark of HarperCollins Christian Publishing, Inc.

Italics in Scripture indicate the author's emphasis.

Unless otherwise noted, Scripture quotations are taken from THE NEW KING JAMES VERSION. © 1982 by Thomas Nelson, Inc. Used by permission. All rights reserved. Scripture quotations marked NIV are from the Holy Bible: New International Version®, NIV®. © 1973, 1978, 1984, 2011 by Biblica, Inc™. Used by permission of Zondervan. All rights reserved worldwide. www.zondervan.com Scripture quotations marked NASB are from NEW AMERICAN STANDARD BIBLE®. © The Lockman Foundation 1960, 1962, 1963, 1968, 1971, 1972, 1973, 1975, 1977, 1995. Used by permission. Scripture quotations marked ESV are from THE ENGLISH STANDARD VERSION. © 2001 by Crossway Bibles, a division of Good News Publishers.

ISBN-13: 978-1-4003-2270-1
ISBN-13: 978-0-529-12087-8 (CU)

Printed in China

15 16 17 18 LEO 6 5 4

Contents

Jesus: Who He Is

Jesus: His Works and His Words

Jesus: His Passion

Jesus: Why He Matters

Introduction

The Son of God stepped out of heaven and entered this world to dwell among us. His ultimate purpose is to rule and receive worship forever, but first He came "to seek and to save the lost" (Luke 19:10)—to "save His people from their sins" (Matthew 1:21). Specifically, He came to die in order to offer His own life as a sacrifice for undeserving sinners. He came "[not] to be served, but to serve, and to give His life a ransom for many" (Matthew 20:28).

In order to do that, He entered this world as a helpless infant. He lived a sinless life of perfect obedience under the rigorous demands of Moses' law (Galatians 4:4), while embodying all the perfections of divine holiness. Even though He was subject to normal human vulnerabilities such as hunger, thirst, and weariness (Hebrews 4:15), He triumphantly resisted every temptation that is common to us all (Hebrews 2:18). Setting aside His glory as sovereign Lord of all, He humbled Himself to become a slave for all, suffering the most disgraceful death on a cross—executed as if He had been guilty of capital crimes (Philippians 2:6–11).

When it may have seemed His life and ministry had utterly failed, He gloriously rose from the dead, demonstrating His authority over life and death and His power over all the forces of hell.

Jesus died and rose for His chosen people—those who would believe in Him and confess Him as Lord. On that cross He bore their guilt and suffered the punishment due to them. Having thus atoned in full for their sins, He graciously covers them with His own perfect righteousness (2 Corinthians 5:21) so that they stand before God fully justified. He freely grants us eternal life.

That is the heart of the gospel message, the greatest story ever told. It culminates in the greatest and most gracious invitation ever given: "Let him who thirsts come. Whoever desires, let him take the water of life freely" (Revelation 22:17).

In Jesus Christ we see the fullness of the glory

of God on display. The mystery and majesty of that glory shines brightly for those who have spiritual eyes to see. My prayer for you is that as you read, God will open your eyes to see, your mind to understand, and your heart to embrace the truth about the Lord Jesus Christ. Above all, I pray that you will love the living Savior Himself and receive His gift of eternal life.

For the Master,

Jesus: Who He Is

The eternal, sovereign God came to earth as a human being to live a righteous life among His people and then to die as a perfect sacrifice to deliver from the wrath of God all who repent and believe. With those truths in mind, we dare not trivialize or sentimentalize the persons and events surrounding the birth of Christ. The almighty God of the universe humbly came to earth in human flesh to seek and to save the lost (Matthew 18:11; Luke 19:10; 5:32; Romans 5:8).

His Birth

Why can we believe in the virgin birth of Jesus?

Matthew needs only one verse (1:18) to announce the fact of Christ's virgin birth. Such a concise statement, though it doesn't all by itself prove the point, strongly suggests that the notion of our Lord and Savior's virgin birth was not simply a man-made story. A human author, writing strictly on his own initiative, would characteristically tend to describe such a momentous and amazing event in an expansive, detailed, and elaborate manner. But not the apostle Matthew. He does relate additional circumstances surrounding the virgin birth, but the basic fact is stated in one simple sentence: "After His mother Mary was betrothed to Joseph, before they came together, she was found with child of the Holy Spirit."

How is the virgin birth possible?

Admittedly, all these many centuries after Matthew's divinely inspired gospel declared that Jesus was born of a virgin, His miraculous conception remains impossible to understand by human reason alone. It was a miracle, and there is no natural explanation for it. We don't need a scientific or analytical explanation for it, any more than we need scientific proof of how the intricacies of the universe were created from nothing. Scripture is peppered with miracles and mysterious doctrines. How can God be one being in three persons? How could Christ rise from the dead? We can't even explain precisely what happens when depraved sinners are born again as they repent of their sins and trust Christ. Many of the essentials of Christianity are beyond the capacity of human minds to fathom. That's okay. We can't comprehend infinity either, but no one doubts the concept. Scripture is full of truths that transcend human thoughts. "For who has known the mind of the LORD? Or who has been His counselor?" (Romans 11:34). God wants believers to accept the truth of His Word by faith.

What did Mary model for believers in her response to the news she would be mother to the Son of God?

In Luke 1:34, Mary asked the angel, "How can [I have a son], since I do not know a man?" Mary's question was born out of wonder, not doubt nor disbelief, so the angel did not rebuke her. Then, once she understood a little more clearly, Mary offered a song of praise, known as the Magnificat. Mary refered to God as "Savior," indicating both that she recognized her own need of a Savior and that she knew the true God as her Savior. Mary did not see herself as sinless, nor did she trust in her own good works. Quite the opposite was true; she employed language typical of someone whose only hope for salvation was divine grace. The quality of Mary that shines most clearly through this passage is a deep sense of humility.

Why did Matthew and Luke include such long genealogies in their gospel accounts?

From their earliest days as a people, the Jews considered their ancestry important. They divided the promised land into tribal areas, and within those areas were towns and villages that belonged to certain families who owned land there. Every fifty years the various lands would revert to the original owners, so genealogies were very important.

In addition, these careful, detailed records of their family histories enabled each man to identify his father's home area and go back there for official obligations such as Caesar Augustus's census.

Why are the genealogies in Matthew and Luke different?

- The writers had two different goals. Luke's genealogy, aiming to show Christ as the redeemer of humanity, goes all the way back to Adam (Matthew 1:1–17; Luke 3:23–28). Matthew's purpose is somewhat narrower: to demonstrate that Christ is the King and Messiah of Israel. (Matthew quotes more than sixty times from Old Testament prophetic passages, emphasizing how Christ fulfills all those promises.)
- The two genealogies take different chronological views of Jesus' family tree. Luke goes from the present to the past, beginning with Jesus' grandfather and going all the way back to Adam and God. Matthew, however, approaches matters in the opposite fashion. He goes from the past

to the present, starting with Abraham and ending with Jesus.

- In Matthew, the genealogy is paternal, going through Jesus' earthly father, Joseph; and Joseph's father, Jacob; back to David. In Luke, the genealogy is maternal, going through Jesus' mother, Mary; and Mary's father, Heli; back to David.

- Matthew's paternal genealogy proved that Jesus came from a line that proceeded from David through Solomon. That proof is true even though Jesus was not the human son of Joseph. Because Joseph married Mary, the mother of Jesus, he became the legal father of Jesus. As a result, Jesus received from Joseph the full legal right to the throne of David.

- Luke's maternal genealogy further solidifies Jesus' claim to the throne of David by proving that He has the blood of David in His veins because of His mother, Mary. So, either way, Jesus is a genuine, legitimate descendant of King David.

- In summary, the Messiah is king legally through Joseph and naturally through Mary. His scriptural credentials are thorough, clear, and irrefutable. From every perspective, we can crown Jesus King of kings and Lord of lords.

Why is it significant that Jesus was born in Bethlehem?

All scripturally informed Jews knew certain facts about the Messiah who would one day come to earth. They knew He would come from the royal line of David and reign from the throne in Jerusalem over Israel's glorious kingdom. And one thing about the Messiah that faithful Jews were certain of was set forth by the prophet Micah:

> But you, Bethlehem Ephrathah, though you are little among the thousands of Judah, yet out of you shall come forth to Me the One to be Ruler in Israel, whose goings forth are from of old, from everlasting. (Micah 5:2)

The Romans normally registered people in their current place of residence rather than making them return to their homeland or hometown. But in accord with Jewish custom, Mary and Joseph had to go back to Bethlehem "because [Joseph] was of the house and lineage of David" (Luke 2:4).

So when—according to Luke 2:1—"it came to pass in those days that a decree went out from Caesar Augustus that all the world should be registered," Jesus' parents were providentially directed to be in Bethlehem at precisely the right time to fulfill Micah 5:2. The journey from Nazareth to Bethlehem, however, was a difficult trek of more than seventy miles through mountainous terrain—a particularly grueling journey for Mary, on the verge of delivery.

What do we know about the inn where Mary and Joseph stayed in Bethlehem?

In Luke 2:7, the Greek word for *inn* is not the usual term for *inn*. Instead, Luke used a word that denoted a shelter or place of lodging for guests. It was not an actual inn operated for the feeding and housing of guests. Instead, it was more like the sleeping section of a public shelter or campground.

Typically, such shelters had four sides and two levels, with the top part being like the loft in a barn. One section of the shelter may have had crude doors to close it off if desired. The entire structure would have been quite primitive, the kind of place where travelers could spend one or more nights in the loft area and keep their animals down in the center area, safe from theft. Their goods could be stored in the center as well.

Why does Luke tell us that Mary
"wrapped [the baby Jesus] in
swaddling cloths" (Luke 2:12)?

The ancient custom was to wrap the arms, legs, and body of the baby with long strips of cloth to provide warmth and security. Parents in those days also believed that wrapping the child helped his or her bones to grow straight. Luke's point in mentioning the wrapping cloths, however, is that Mary treated Jesus the way any mother would treat a normal newborn. Physically, He looked like any other child, and His parents treated Him as such. God did not provide Him with royal robes or other fancy clothing, but simply directed Mary and Joseph to welcome Him as they would any other beloved child. (The absence of swaddling cloths was a sign of poverty or lack of parental care [Ezekiel 16:4].)

So what exactly did Mary lay her swaddled baby in?

A more literal translation of the Greek word for *manger* is "feeding trough." From that we can further deduce that Joseph and Mary were staying in the section of the shelter that accommodated travelers' animals.

When Christ entered the world, He came to a place that had some of the smelliest, filthiest, and most uncomfortable conditions. But that is part of the wonder of divine grace, isn't it? When the Son of God came down from heaven, He came all the way down. He did not hang on to His equality with God; rather, He set it aside for a time and completely humbled Himself (Philippians 2:5–8).

Furthermore, the picture of the infant Son of God tolerating a stable's dirt and foul odors is a fitting metaphor for the later scene of the Savior bearing the stench of sin as He died at Calvary. What an amazing picture!

Is it odd that the shepherds were the very first people to hear about Jesus' birth?

The Lord's preference for the lowly is seen at the very beginning of the Gospels, reflected in the angels' bringing the good news of the Savior's birth to shepherds, some of the commonest and most unappreciated of laborers in Jewish society. When Jesus came, He did not go first of all to the people of prestige, influence, and clout. He went first to the poor and lowly, the meek and afflicted—anyone who was outcast—and the shepherds fit that category.

How were shepherds regarded in that time and place?

Shepherding was not a shameful profession, just a lowly one that included many menial tasks. Shepherds were basically an insignificant class of workers, poorly educated and poorly paid. In fact, because it did not require much skill, the task of shepherding was often given to children. On the Jewish social ladder, though, shepherds were the lowest people because they had to care for sheep seven days a week. That work schedule meant they could not observe the Sabbath the way Mosaic law dictated. Neither could shepherds keep the myriad fastidious, man-made regulations the Pharisees had foisted on top of the law. Such legalism confounded most of the common Jews, and certainly the shepherds couldn't abide by all those rules either. Therefore, to one degree or another, people viewed shepherds as outcasts because they violated religious law. In fact, as the strict legalism of the Pharisees grew and permeated more and more of Jewish society, shepherds became more despised than ever. In the minds of some, they were stereotyped unreliable, dishonest, unsavory characters, guilty of sheep stealing and many other illegal activities.

What was significant about the angel's announcement, "Unto you is born this day in the city of David a Savior, who is Christ the Lord" (Luke 2:11 ESV)?

First, Jesus' being called the Christ indicates that He is God's anointed King. He is the eternal King of kings who will sit on David's throne and reign over His Kingdom forever. Also, when the angel called Jesus "Lord," he was using a divine designation and claiming that the child in Bethlehem was God. To say that Jesus is Lord is to say that He is first and foremost God. In fact, it is the most fundamental and essential confession of the Christian faith. It is unequivocal that if any person desires to be saved, he must make the heartfelt and vocal confession that Jesus is Lord (Romans 10:9).

In addition to that, the expression "Jesus is Lord" implies all the sovereignty and authority associated with one who is God. For "Lord" in Luke 2:11, the angel used the Greek word *kurios*, which expresses an authority that is valid and lawful. The ultimate lawful authority in the universe, of course, is God. So the angel was saying Jesus is lawfully Lord because of who He is, the Son of God. The Greek translators of the Old Testament and the writers of the New Testament used *kurios* so often to refer to God that it became synonymous for the name of God. So when the angel declared Jesus to be Lord, he was declaring Him to be the true God, the one who possesses all authority and sovereignty.

If the angel's announcement was more significant than a first glance suggests, what is the full meaning of the heavenly host's words of praise: "Glory to God in the highest, and on earth peace, goodwill toward men!" (Luke 2:14)?

First, "on earth peace" does not refer to peace of mind, rest for the weary, or absence of wars. The angels meant peace with God that results from genuine salvation. Because His Son has brought reconciliation, we no longer need to be God's enemies. The angels were praising the Father, giving Him glory in heaven, because He sent salvation down to earth in the person of Jesus Christ.

The second phrase, "goodwill toward men," also deserves an accurate understanding. For decades people have used this phrase out of context and trivialized it to mean pleasant sentiments at Christmas or kind words and deeds extended to others. Those thoughts are not what the angels had in mind. Both the New King James Version, "goodwill toward men," and the New American Standard Bible, "with whom He is pleased," sound as though God is going to grant spiritual peace to those who deserve it or earn it. But an alternate reading makes the meaning more clear: "Peace among men of His good pleasure." Men and women do not earn God's peace, but He gives it to them because He is pleased to do so.

What is commendable about the shepherds' response to this good news proclaimed from the heavens?

No one had to prod the shepherds into the right response to the divine messengers' words. They were in full agreement that nothing would deter them from going immediately to find the newly arrived Savior: "Let us go straight to Bethlehem then, and see this thing that has happened which the Lord has made known to us" (Luke 2:15 NASB). Since Bethlehem sits on a ridge, the shepherds most likely had to walk uphill the two miles from the fields to town. So as soon as possible, they set out to "see this thing that has happened."

The word translated *thing* in this passage denotes much more in Greek than it does in English. The term literally means "word" or "reality." The shepherds understood that they had received a word from God, and the reality of it was that the

Messiah had been born that same day. And the reality was something they could confirm tangibly because the angel gave them a sign to look for, a baby wrapped in cloths and lying in a manger (Luke 2:12). The shepherds had seen and believed the angels, which was sufficient verification for what had occurred, but they wanted to obtain additional authentication by finding the child exactly where the first angel said He would be. That would affirm their eagerness of faith and prove that they were participants in more than a mere earthly drama.

When the Magi arrived at the home of Jesus—a toddler at that point— they brought gifts as an act of worship. What is the significance of gold, frankincense, and myrrh?

As an expression of the Magi's grateful worship, "they presented gifts to Him: gold, frankincense, and myrrh" (Matthew 2:11). *Gold* had long been and still is the universal symbol of material wealth and value. It was also a symbol of nobility and royalty, and thus the Magi were appropriately giving Christ the King royal gifts of gold. *Frankincense* was an expensive, sweet-smelling incense used for only the most special occasions. Traditionally, it was the incense of deity. *Myrrh* was a valuable perfume that some interpreters say represented the gift for a mortal. Therefore its role among the Magi's gifts was to underscore Christ's humanity.

Why did Jesus, the Son of God, need to be circumcised?

The circumcision was necessary because Jesus needed to obey God's Law in its entirety and fulfill all righteousness. Jesus would be a man in every sense, and therefore He would fulfill all the requirements listed in the Law for God's people (Matthew 3:15). Even before His Son could consciously comply, God the Father made sure that Jesus' earthly parents fulfilled every Old Testament requirement for His life. Jesus' circumcision was simply a preview to what Luke envisioned when he later wrote, "And Jesus increased in wisdom and stature, and in favor with God and men" (Luke 2:52).

Why did Joseph and Mary present Jesus at the temple?

As with the circumcision and purification, Joseph and Mary were obeying the Old Testament law when they presented their Son to God: "The firstborn of your sons you shall give to Me" (Exodus 22:29; also 13:2, 12, 15; Numbers 8:17). It was not mandatory for them to go to the Temple to present Jesus. But in the spirit of how Hannah brought Samuel to the Lord (1 Samuel 1:24–28), Joseph and Mary went above and beyond the normal duty and brought God's Son to God's house. They knew the child was very special and that He, of all children, belonged to the Lord already. By their action Jesus' parents in effect said, "We are devoting this Child to You, God. He is already Yours, so do whatever You will in His life so He serves, honors, and glorifies You."

That special presentation did not mean, however, that Joseph and Mary dedicated Jesus to the

Levitical priesthood. They were of the tribe of Judah and therefore, like all non-Levite families and according to the law, they needed to redeem their Son from that priestly responsibility by paying five shekels of silver (Numbers 18:15–16). That would have been equivalent to many days' wages, a difficult amount for a working-class couple like Joseph and Mary to pay. But God made sure they had the necessary coins.

That Jesus the Redeemer was ceremonially redeemed is both an interesting irony and an important scriptural reality. Just as with His earlier circumcision and later baptism, Jesus did not need to go through any kind of redemption. He was the sinless Son of God; He did not need to be cleansed from sin or redeemed from condemnation. But He was circumcised, He was baptized, and He was "redeemed" as part of His presentation to God—all because He had to obey the letter of the Law to fulfill all righteousness on our behalf.

His Youth

What do we know about Jesus' childhood?

Luke 2 presents the one authentic biblical account of Jesus' childhood, and the scene reveals a very normal boy with true-to-life parents. Joseph and Mary were traveling with a large caravan of friends and relatives from Nazareth to celebrate the Passover in Jerusalem. No doubt hundreds of people from their community went together to the feast. Men and women in such a group might have been separated by some distance, and it appears each parent thought Jesus was with the other. Jesus' separation from His parents was rooted in this very simple misunderstanding. The gospel account by no means suggests that Jesus was being mischievous or rebellious.

He was simply engrossed in the goings-on at the temple. On the day they were scheduled to depart, however, Jesus' parents were preoccupied with preparations for the journey home. When they left, He lingered—not out of disrespect or defiance, but simply because (like all children) He was utterly absorbed in something that had arrested His attention. His true humanness never shows more clearly than it does in this account.

Why did it take Joseph and Mary so long to realize their son was missing?

Because so many pilgrims descended on Jerusalem during that week, all the roads and inns would have been jammed, and large numbers of people from each community would travel to and from the feast together. From a town the size of Nazareth, there may have been a hundred or more people in Jesus' parents' party, some walking, some riding slow beasts of burden. A band that large would likely stretch over a mile's distance, and the women generally traveled in a group or several small groups together, rather than being spread out among the men. So it is easy to understand how this confusion arose. Mary and Joseph no doubt each presumed Jesus was with the other parent. He certainly would not have been a mischief-prone child, so neither parent gave any thought to investigating His whereabouts until the end of the first day's travel, when they suddenly discovered He was not with the group at all.

What was happening in the temple when Jesus' parents found Him?

This is a unique picture of Jesus, seated among Israel's leading rabbis, politely listening to them, asking questions, and amazing them with His comprehension and discernment. Still a child in every sense, He was already the most amazing student they had ever had the privilege to teach. He had evidently kept these teachers fully engaged for three days, and when Joseph and Mary finally came upon the scene, Jesus' attention was still so focused on the lesson that He had not yet even thought to go looking for them. Because He was still a child—the perfect child—it is only reasonable to assume that Jesus maintained the role of a respectful student.

We're not to think Jesus was rebuking, challenging, even instructing those rabbis. In fact, Luke seems to include this brief vignette about Jesus' childhood precisely to stress the full humanity of

Christ—how He grew "in wisdom and stature, and in favor with God and men" (Luke 2:52). Again, Luke is saying that every aspect of Jesus' development into full manhood (intellectually, physically, spiritually, and socially) was ordinary, not extraordinary. Even though He was God incarnate, with all the full attributes of God in His infinite being, Jesus fully submitted the use of those attributes (like His divine omniscience) to His Father's will. Consequently, there were times when Jesus' omniscience was put on display (Matthew 9:4; John 2:24). At other times, however, His knowledge was veiled by His humanity according to the Father's purpose (Mark 13:32). In His incarnation, as Luke explained here, Jesus experienced the normal process of human growth, including intellectual development. All of that was part of the Father's perfect plan for His Son.

According to Luke, Jesus was listening and asking questions, and what amazed these tutors was His grasp of the information they were giving Him as well as His answers (Luke 2:47). So the rabbis were obviously quizzing Him as they went, and they were astonished at both His attention span and His ability to perceive spiritual truth. The questions Jesus asked those rabbis were part of His learning process, not some backhanded way of showing up the rabbis. He was truly learning from them and processing what they taught Him. This experience surely provided our Lord's first personal insight into their approach to Scripture and their religious system, which He would later denounce.

What happened when Jesus' parents found Him?

Jesus' lesson in the temple came to a rather abrupt halt when Joseph and Mary finally found their Son. Their anxiety and exasperation are certainly easy to understand from any parent's point of view: "When they saw Him, they were amazed; and His mother said to Him, 'Son, why have You done this to us? Look, Your father and I have sought You anxiously'" (Luke 2:48).

This was probably not the first time—and it certainly would not be the last—that Jesus' innocent motives would be misunderstood and misconstrued. Nor should His reply to Joseph and Mary be read as an insolent retort. Jesus was truly amazed that they hadn't known exactly where to look for Him. "He said to them, 'Why did you seek Me? Did you not know that I must be about My Father's business?'" (Luke 2:49). Mary, of course, was referring to Joseph when she said "your father." Jesus, however, was calling God "My Father." (Plainly Jesus already had a clear sense of who He was and where His true accountability lay.) But at the moment, Jesus' parents were so overwhelmed with relief to have found Him, so amazed to find Him at the feet of these prominent rabbis, and so fatigued from the whole ordeal that "they did not understand the statement which He spoke to them" (Luke 2:50).

Luke ended this singular glimpse at Jesus' childhood with this wrap-up:

> Then He went down with them and came to Nazareth, and was subject to them, but His mother kept all these things in her heart. And Jesus increased in wisdom and stature, and in favor with God and men. (Luke 2:51–52)

That is the end of Luke 2, and it is a perfect summary of Jesus' boyhood.

Since Jesus is God, why did He have to learn anything?

Initially, we don't readily understand how Jesus, as God incarnate, with all the attributes of deity, could possibly increase in wisdom or gain favor with God. But this is a statement about Jesus' humanity. As God, Jesus is of course perfect in every way and therefore eternally unchanging (Hebrews 13:8). Divine omniscience, by definition, does not allow for any increase in wisdom. But in the conscious awareness of His human mind, Jesus did not always avail Himself of the infinite knowledge He possessed as God. He did not lose His omniscience or cease being God, but He voluntarily suspended the use of that quality—so that as a boy, He learned things the same way every human child learns.

Furthermore, in His growth from boyhood to manhood, Jesus gained the admiration of others and the approval of God for the way He lived as a human subject to God's law (Galatians 4:4). Luke 2:52 is therefore not a denial of Jesus' deity; it is an affirmation of His true humanity. The stress is on the normalcy of His development. In His progress from childhood to manhood, Jesus endured everything any other child would experience—except for the guilt of sin.

Why do we sometimes see Jesus' omniscience and sometimes we don't?

Jesus did not cease being God or divest Himself of divine attributes in order to become man. Rather, He took on a human nature (an addition, not a subtraction) and submitted the use of His divine attributes to the will of the Father (Philippians 2:5–8). Therefore, there were times when His omniscience was on display (Matthew 9:4; John 2:24–25; 4:17–18; 11:11–14; 16:30) and other times when it was veiled by His humanity in accordance with the Father's will (Mark 13:32). Christ was therefore subject to the normal process of human growth—intellectually, physically, spiritually, and socially.

Why did Jesus need to be born of a virgin?

Simply put, if Jesus had not been both human and divine, there would be no gospel. In other words, had Jesus been conceived by natural means, with Joseph or anyone else as His father, He would not have been God and therefore would not have been a true Savior of sinners. To be in accord with what Scripture reported about His life, Jesus would have had to make false claims about Himself, and He would have had to endorse false stories or hoaxes concerning the resurrection and ascension. Meanwhile everyone would have remained spiritually dead, condemned forever by their unforgiven sins.

Luke 2 is a key account of Jesus' birth, but what does the book of Hebrews teach about the God-man born in Bethlehem?

The letter to the Hebrews, written about AD 67 to 69 by an unidentified author, was obviously written to Jews, mostly true believers in Jesus. Its purpose was to show them that Jesus Christ is in fact the fulfillment of all the Old Testament messianic promises and that He is superior to all the pictures, types, representations, and shadows that preceded Him. The epistle was written to assure believing Jews that their faith was rightly placed and to encourage unbelieving Jews that embracing Jesus was the right commitment to make. Many in the community were intellectually convinced Jesus was the Messiah and God, but they had not yet personally believed and publicly confessed Him as Lord. They didn't want to be alienated like their believing friends had been. Some had been put out of the synagogue, some had been ostracized by their families, and others had lost their jobs. The writer affirms that the babe born in Bethlehem is the Messiah and that He is indeed the Lord of a New Covenant, which is far superior to the Old Covenant of Moses.

What seven truths about Christ's preeminence are set forth in Hebrews 1:2–3?

The letter to the Hebrews opens with an insightful, divine description of who the baby born in Bethlehem really is. It is probably the most concise and comprehensive New Testament summary statement of the superiority of Christ:

> God, who at various times and in various ways spoke in time past to the fathers by the prophets, has in these last days spoken to us by His Son, whom He has appointed heir of all things, through whom also He made the worlds; who being the brightness of His glory and the express image of His person, and upholding all things by the word of His power, when He had by Himself purged our sins, sat down at the right hand of the Majesty on high. (Hebrews 1:1–3)

Let's unpack this.

- **Christ is the heir of all things:** God has planned for Jesus ultimately to inherit absolutely everything. This plan adheres to Jewish inheritance laws that said the firstborn child received the wealth of the family's estate.
- **Christ is the agent of creation:** The Greek word rendered *worlds* in Hebrews 1:2 does not mean the material world but "the ages," as it is usually translated elsewhere. Christ created not only the physical earth but also time, space, energy, and every variety of matter. He effortlessly created the entire universe and finished it as something good.
- **Christ possesses the brightness of God's glory:** *Brightness*, which may also be translated *radiance* (NASB) and literally means "to send forth light," indicates that Jesus is the manifestation of God to us. Just as the sun's rays illuminate and warm the earth, Christ is God's glorious light that shines into the hearts of people.

- **Christ is the essence of God:** Jesus has all the attributes that are indispensable to who and what God is, such as immutability (unchangeableness), omniscience, omnipotence, and omnipresence. He is the exact stamp or replication of God. In the words of the Nicene Creed, Jesus Christ is "very God of very God."

- **Christ has ultimate authority:** Christ makes the universe a cosmos instead of chaos. He infallibly ensures that the universe runs as an ordered, reliable unit instead of as an erratic, unpredictable muddle. That's because our Lord has devised and implemented the myriad natural laws, both complex and straightforward, that are all perfectly reliable, consistent, and precisely suited to their particular purposes. Time and again they wonderfully demonstrate the mind and power of Jesus Christ working through the universe. The whole universe hangs on His powerful arm, His infinite wisdom, and His ability to control every element and orchestrate the movements of every molecule, atom, and subatomic particle.

- **Christ removes our sins:** The Old Testament priests offered animal sacrifices over and over, but none of those could ultimately remove the people's sins. Those repeated sacrifices instead merely pointed to the desperate need for a once-for-all sacrifice that could finally take away sins. And God provided such a sacrifice in the person of Jesus. This final new covenant sacrifice had to be a perfect, sinless substitute. To pay the price of sin for others, that person had to be perfect or he would have had to pay the price for his own sin. And since no one in the world is without sin, the substitute had to be someone from outside the world. Yet he still needed to be a man to die in the place of men and women. Of course, the only person who could meet those requirements was Jesus Christ. He was the sinless man who could be the perfect substitute for sinners. Once and for all He paid the price for sins for everyone who would ever believe in Him.

- **Christ is exalted in heaven:** When Jesus went into heaven, He did what no Old Testament priest did—He sat down. Priests never sat down while ministering because their work was never done. But Christ's work was done; He had accomplished the work of redemption on the cross, and therefore it was appropriate for Him to sit down. He remains on the right hand of the throne of God as the believer's great High Priest and Intercessor (Hebrews 7:25; 9:24).

Why is it valuable to read Hebrews 1 in conjunction with Luke 2?

An analysis of Hebrews 1:1–14 is a fitting capstone to a discussion of the birth of Christ. It ensures that when you consider the baby in the Bethlehem shelter, you don't merely see an adorable child who grew up to be a good teacher and compassionate healer. The passage points you beyond that to an accurate understanding of the person and work of Christ. The writer, through careful, Spirit-inspired argumentation, declares irrefutably that the child born to Mary was indeed God in the manger. He truly was the Son of God, miraculously conceived by the Holy Spirit yet born naturally to a woman in Israel. And without doubt He was the Lord and Savior who lived a perfect life and died as a perfect sacrifice so that all who believe in Him might have eternal life.

Jesus: His Works and His Words

Just as God's hand was clear in the miracles surrounding Jesus' birth—His conception, His birth in Bethlehem, the appearance of the angel and the heavenly host, the shepherds being the first to know of the Messiah's arrival to this dark planet—God's power was made manifest in Jesus' works and words throughout His ministry on earth. His miracles and teachings, however, generated not only love and devotion but also hate and scorn.

Preparing
the Way

God sent John the Baptist to
prepare the way for Jesus.
What was John's message?

Johns preaching can be summed up with:
"Repent, for the kingdom of heaven is at hand!"
(Matthew 3:2). And people responded: "Jerusalem,
all Judea, and all the region around the Jordan
went out to [John] and were baptized by him in the
Jordan, confessing their sins" (Matthew 3:5–6).
John spoke of repentance as a radical turning from
sin that inevitably became manifest in the fruit of
righteousness.

Why did Jesus have to be baptized by John (Matthew 3:13–17)?

Through His baptism, Christ identified with sinners, for He would ultimately bear our sins; His perfect righteousness would be imputed to us (2 Corinthians 5:21). The act of baptism was a necessary part of the righteousness He secured for sinners. This first public event of Jesus' ministry is rich in meaning: (1) it pictures His death and resurrection; (2) it prefigures the significance of Christian baptism; (3) it marks Jesus' first public identification with those whose sins He would bear; and (4) it affirms His messiahship publicly by testimony directly from heaven (see p. 52).

What confirmation that Jesus was the Messiah did John witness?

According to Matthew, "the heavens were opened" as Jesus came up from the water of His baptism. At that moment, Jesus "saw the Spirit of God descending like a dove and alighting upon Him. And suddenly a voice came from heaven, saying, 'This is My beloved Son, in whom I am well pleased'" (Matthew 3:16–17). Here all three persons of the Trinity are clearly expressed. The Father's declaration of love for His Son and the Spirit's empowerment officially inaugurate Christ's ministry.

Why was John later confused by Jesus' ministry?

John was understandably confused by the turn of events: he was imprisoned while Christ carried on a ministry of healing, not judgment, in Galilee, far from Jerusalem, the city of the king— and not finding a completely warm reception there. John wondered if he had misunderstood Jesus' agenda. It would be wrong to interpret this as a wavering of his faith, though.

Miracles

Healing the Leper

Three gospels tell of Jesus healing a leper (Matthew 8:2; Mark 1:40; Luke 5:12). Why was healing this particular disease significant?

The leper's healing emphasizes Jesus' miraculous power over disease, since leprosy was one of the most dreaded diseases of antiquity. Lepers were considered ceremonially unclean and were outcast from society (Leviticus 13:11). While the Old Testament term for leprosy includes other skin diseases, this man may have actually had true leprosy (Hansen's disease), or else his cure would not have created such a sensation (Mark 1:45).

What makes Mark's account of this cleansing of a leper distinct from the others?

Only Mark records Jesus' emotional reaction to the leper's desperate plight: "Jesus, moved with compassion, stretched out His hand and touched him" (Mark 1:41). Unlike rabbis, who avoided lepers lest they become ceremonially defiled, Jesus expressed His compassion with a physical gesture.

Why did Jesus command the leper to "show yourself to the priest" (Mark 1:44)?

The priest was the one on duty in the temple. Jesus commanded the healed leper to observe the Old Testament regulations concerning cleansed lepers (Leviticus 14:1–32). Until the required offerings had been made, the man remained ceremonially unclean. The priest's acceptance of the man's offering would be public affirmation of his cure and cleansing.

Why did Jesus not want word about such healings to spread?

When Jesus healed the leper, He specifically said, "Say nothing to anyone" (Mark 1:44 NASB). Jesus knew that the ensuing publicity would hinder His ability to minister and divert attention away from His message—and that is exactly what happened. (Only Mark records the leper's disobedience, although Luke hints at it [Luke 5:15].) The result of the leper's disobedience was that Jesus could no longer enter a city without being mobbed by those seeking to be cured of diseases. Jesus' ministry of teaching in that area thus came to a halt (Mark 1:45).

An Amazing Catch of Fish

What happened one morning when Jesus the carpenter coached His disciples, who were fishermen, about catching fish (Luke 5:1–11)?

At Jesus' early-morning command to let down the nets again, Simon answered and said to Him, "Master, we have toiled all night and caught nothing; nevertheless at Your word I will let down the net." The disciples obeyed and "caught a great number of fish, and their net was breaking. So they signaled to their partners in the other boat to come and help them. And they came and filled both the boats, so that they began to sink" (Luke 5:5–7). The remarkable catch of fish was clearly a miracle, astonishing to all the fishermen in Capernaum. Simon Peter immediately realized he was in the presence of the Holy One exercising His divine power, and he was stricken with shame over his own sin.

Calming the Storm

What kind of storm did Jesus calm (Matthew 8:23; Mark 4:35; Luke 8:22)?

Jesus and His disciples were on the western shore of the Sea of Galilee. To escape the crowds for a brief respite, Jesus wanted to go to the eastern shore, which had no large cities and therefore fewer people. Wind occurs commonly on that lake, which is about 690 feet below sea level and surrounded by hills. The Greek word for *storm* can also mean "whirlwind." In this case, it was a storm so severe that it took on the properties of a hurricane.

What was the disciples' reaction to the storm—and to Jesus' ability to calm the storm?

The disciples themselves, who were used to being on the lake in the wind, thought this storm would drown them. Yet Jesus was so exhausted from a full day of healing and preaching that even this storm could not wake Him up. Storms normally subside gradually, but when the Creator gave the order, the natural elements of this storm ceased immediately. Jesus' calming the storm demonstrates His unlimited power over the natural world. At that point, then, the disciples felt not a fear of being harmed by the storm, but a reverence for the supernatural power Jesus had just displayed. The only thing more terrifying than having a storm outside the boat was having God in the boat!

The Paralytic by the Pool at Bethesda

John alone tells of Jesus healing this paralyzed man (John 5:1–15). Why is this included in Scripture?

In the scope of Jesus' whole ministry, this might have seemed a fairly unremarkable healing. It wasn't accompanied by any sermon or public discourse. Jesus simply spoke privately and very briefly with this one infirm man in a context so crowded that few people, if any, were likely to notice. There was no fanfare prior to the healing, and John's description of the incident gives us no reason to think the man's healing resulted in any public spectacle. Jesus had healed countless people before, and in that light, everything about this incident was more or less routine for the ministry of Jesus. Except for one detail. John closes verse 9 by noting, "And that day was the Sabbath" (for a more complete discussion, see the next question).

Why is this detail—"that day was the Sabbath"—significant?

At first glance, that statement may appear to be an

incidental background fact. But it is actually the turning point of the narrative, sparking a conflict that would mark yet another escalation of hostility between Jesus and the chief religious leaders of Israel. By the end of that day, their contempt for Him would have been ratcheted to such a level of pure hatred that from then on they would not rest—or let Him rest—until they had completely eliminated Him.

Remember that matters concerning obedience on the Sabbath were the Pharisees' home turf. Jesus knew full well that they were fanatical about it. They had invented all kinds of restrictions for the day of rest, adding their own superstrict rules to Moses' law in the name of tradition. They treated their man-made customs as if they were binding law, equal in authority to the revealed word of God. The Pharisees did the same thing with all the law's ceremonial precepts, going far beyond what Scripture required. They made every ritual as elaborate and every ordinance as restrictive as possible. They believed this was a pathway to greater holiness.

The Paralytic Lowered
Through the Roof

When the paralytic's friends lowered him between the beams to Jesus' feet, Jesus didn't comment on the obvious—the roof or the paralysis. Why did Jesus first address the man's sins?

Christ addressed the man's greater need first: "Man, your sins are forgiven" (Luke 5:20). In doing so, Jesus asserted a prerogative that was God's alone. His subsequent healing of the man's paralysis was proof that He had the authority to forgive sins as well as heal physical infirmities and illness. Jesus' ability to heal anyone and everyone at will—totally and immediatly (Luke 5:25)—was incontrovertible proof of His deity. As God, Jesus had all authority to forgive sins. This decisive moment should have ended the Pharisees' opposition once and for all. Instead, they tried to discredit Jesus by charging Him with violating their Sabbath rules. This response is curiously noncommittal, not void of wonder and amazement, but utterly void of true faith.

Jesus raised His friend Lazarus from the dead. What was significant about the words of the dead man's sister Martha when Lazarus still lay in the grave?

When Jesus heard the news of His friend's death, He delayed going to the grave. (The delay of four days ensured that no one could misinterpret the miracle as a fraud or mere resuscitation.) Martha first said to Jesus upon His arrival, "Lord, if You had been here, my brother would not have died. But even now I know that whatever You ask of God, God will give You" (John 11:21–22). Martha's words were not a rebuke of Jesus, but a testimony of her trust in His healing power. Martha was not saying that she believed Jesus could raise Lazarus from the dead, but that she knew He had a special relationship to God so that His prayers could bring some good from this sad story.

With this miracle, Jesus authenticated His claims to be the Messiah and Son of God. No resurrection or eternal life exists outside of the Son of God. Time is no barrier to the one who has the power of resurrection and life for He can give life at any time.

The Feeding of the Five Thousand

What miracle is recorded in all four Gospels?
The story of the feeding of the five thousand is the only miracle recorded in all four Gospels. John's account of this miracle emphasized the creative power of Christ and decisively supported John's aim to demonstrate the deity of Jesus (John 6:1–14). Consider some of the details: The number of men was five thousand, not including women and children, who probably brought the total up to twenty thousand. "Sheep not having a shepherd" (Mark 6:34) is an Old Testament picture used to describe the people as helpless and starving, lacking in spiritual guidance and protection, and exposed to the perils of sin and spiritual destruction. The disciples ask Jesus, "Shall we go and buy two hundred denarii worth of bread and give them something to eat?" (Mark 6:37). A single denarius was equivalent to a day's pay for the day laborer. Two hundred denarii would therefore equal eight months' wages and be quite beyond the disciples' means.

What was the crowd's response to Jesus' miraculous provision for their empty stomachs?

These people desired a Messiah who met their physical, rather than spiritual, needs. They wanted an earthly, political Messiah to meet all their needs and to deliver them from Roman oppression. Their reaction typifies many who want a "Christ" who makes no demands of them, but of whom they can make their selfish personal requests. "Give us this bread always" (John 6:34) implies that they wanted Jesus to produce food from heaven every day from then on—like a genie who would magically grant them any wish that struck their fancy. After all, they suggested, that's very much like what Moses did for the Israelites in the wilderness: the manna came every day. These people were basically offering to make a deal with Jesus: they would believe in Him if He would agree to make food for them from now on, whenever they demanded it.

What was Jesus' response to their proposal?

Jesus' feeding of the five thousand set the stage for what has come to be known as the "Bread of Life discourse." Jesus said to them, "I am the bread of life. He who comes to Me shall never hunger" (John 6:35). If the multitudes had shown the least bit of interest in hearing the truth, they would have sought clarification of what they did not understand. Instead, "the Jews therefore quarreled among themselves, saying, 'How can this Man give us His flesh to eat?'" (John 6:52). (John regularly used the expression "the Jews" to signify the hostile religious leaders. They were apparently at the head of this crowd.) Notice that Jesus did not stop them at that point and say, "No, you misunderstand. Let Me explain what I mean." They had shown no interest in understanding Jesus, so He persisted with His difficult analogy.

Why were the disciples excited when Jesus began to do miracles like the handful we've looked at?

When Jesus began to do miracles, the disciples must have been ecstatic. Here was undeniable proof that Jesus was the true Messiah! They believed that when Messiah came, He would quickly take authority over all earthly kingdoms and establish His millennial rule worldwide, with Israel as the seat of that kingdom. As a matter of fact, the disciples retained that expectation even after the resurrection, virtually until the ascension of Christ (Acts 1:6).

In addition to the miracles He did, Jesus drew attention to Himself when He overturned the money changers' tables in the temple. Why did He do that?

Bleating sheep, bawling oxen, haggling merchants, and indignant pilgrims all raised their voices together amid the miasma of manure from all those animals. The temple was a hive of noise, dissonance, filth, and pandemonium. It was certainly no atmosphere for worship. It was carnal chaos, the first sight to greet every pilgrim arriving on the temple mount. Jesus' response actually reflects an amazing degree of patience and deliberation. He carefully, painstakingly braided some cords together to make a whip or a scourge. Small cords would be lying around in abundance—cheap strands used to tether the animals. He thus used the tools of the sinners' unjust trade to measure out justice against them.

How did Jesus handle Himself in the fray?

When Jesus turned over the money changers' tables and poured their coins onto the ground, there must have been great tumult all around. But in the midst of it, Jesus appears unruffled—fierce in His anger, perhaps, but resolute, single-minded, stoic, and wholly composed. He is the very picture of self-control. (This is truly righteous indignation, not a violent temper that has gotten out of hand.) The merchants and money changers, by contrast, were instantly sent scrambling. Jesus' decisiveness and power were impressive and must have been incredibly intimidating. His anger is evident; His zeal is grand and imposing; and the force of divine authority in His words is unmistakable.

Jesus didn't hesitate to confront the Jews about their conduct in the temple. What did Jesus do in response to the way the Jews were observing the Sabbath?

T he first major conflict over the Sabbath broke out in the wake of a quiet Sabbath healing at the pool of Bethesda. Almost as soon as the healed man picked up his bed (for the first time in thirty-eight years) and began to walk away, he met some religious leaders who accused him of breaking the Sabbath. Before the day was over, Jesus would justify His own breaking of the Pharisees' Sabbath restrictions by saying He was God's Son and therefore perfectly free to do what God Himself does on the Sabbath.

Why were the Pharisees so adamant about how the Sabbath should be observed?

Ultrastrict legalism had become the defining cultural emblem of life and religion in Israel. Jesus, however, refused to bow to the Pharisees' man-made rules. He broke their Sabbaths openly, repeatedly, and deliberately. He taught that "the Sabbath was made for man, and not man for the Sabbath" (Mark 2:27). Jesus said simply, "My Father has been working until now, and I have been working" (John 5:17). In other words, God Himself is not bound by any Sabbath restrictions. He continues His labors day and night (Psalm 121:4; Isaiah 27:3). Jesus was claiming the same prerogative for Himself. It was tantamount to saying He was Lord of the Sabbath. It was indeed a claim that only God incarnate could righteously make. The religious leaders got the message instantly. Their mood took a turn for the worse: "Therefore the Jews sought all the more to kill Him, because He not only broke the Sabbath, but also said that God was His Father, making Himself equal with God" (John 5:18).

Teachings

In Matthew 5:3–13, Jesus opens His Sermon on the Mount with what has come to be called the Beatitudes. What are the Beatitudes all about?

*B*lessed literally means "happy, fortunate, blissful." Here it speaks of more than surface emotion. Jesus describes the divinely bestowed well-being that belongs only to the faithful. The Beatitudes demonstrate the way to heavenly blessedness. In other words, the eight beatitudes in Matthew's account together describe the true nature of saving faith.

- First, the "poor in spirit" (Matthew 5:3) are those who know they have no spiritual resources of their own.

- "Those who mourn" (Matthew 5:4) are repentant people, truly sorrowful over their own sin.
- "The meek" (Matthew 5:5) are those who truly fear God and know their own unworthiness in light of His holiness.
- "Those who hunger and thirst for righteousness" (Matthew 5:6) are those who, having turned from sin, yearn for what God loves instead.

Those four beatitudes are all inward qualities of authentic faith. They describe the believer's state of heart. More specifically, they describe how the believer sees himself before God: poor, sorrowful, meek, and hungry.

The final four beatitudes describe the outward manifestations of those qualities. They focus mainly on the believer's moral character, and they describe what the authentic Christian should look like to an objective observer.

- "The merciful" (Matthew 5:7) are those

who, as beneficiaries of God's grace, extend grace to others.

- "The pure in heart" (Matthew 5:8) describes people whose thoughts and actions are characterized by holiness.
- "The peacemakers" (Matthew 5:9) speaks mainly of those who spread the message of "peace with God through our Lord Jesus Christ" (Romans 5:1)—which is the only true and lasting peace.
- And obviously, "those who are persecuted for righteousness' sake" (Matthew 5:10) are citizens of Christ's kingdom who suffer because of their affiliation with Him and their faithfulness to Him. The world hates them because it hates Him (John 15:18; 1 John 3:1, 13).

The order is significant. The more faithfully a person lives out the first seven beatitudes, the more he or she will experience the persecution spoken of in the eighth.

What was unsettling, if not radical, about Jesus' Beatitudes?

Each one of these eight qualities is radically at odds with the world's values. The world esteems pride more than humility; loves merriment rather than mourning; thinks strong-willed assertiveness is superior to true meekness; and prefers the satiety of carnal pleasure over a thirst for real righteousness. The world looks with utter contempt on holiness and purity of heart, scorns every plea to make peace with God, and constantly persecutes the truly righteous. Jesus could hardly have devised a list of virtues more at odds with His culture—or ours.

Why did the Beatitudes upset the Pharisees, the key religious leaders of Jesus' day?

In the Sermon on the Mount—which begins with the Beatitudes—Jesus gave us the starting point for imitating God. We need to mourn over our sin with a broken and contrite spirit. When we are overwhelmed by our sinfulness, we will hunger and thirst for righteousness. So there is a paradox: we are to be like God, yet we must know we cannot be like Him on our own.

Yet spiritual self-sufficiency defined the Pharisees' whole system. They refused to acknowledge their sin, much less mourn over it. Far from being meek, they were the very embodiment of stubborn, overbearing self-assertiveness. They didn't hunger and thirst for righteousness; they actually thought they had perfected it. They were not merciful but specialized in "bind[ing] heavy burdens, hard to bear, and lay[ing] them on men's shoulders; but they themselves [would] not move them with one of their fingers" (Matthew 23:4). Their hearts were impure, not pure, and Jesus confronted them about that regularly (Matthew 23:27). They were spiritual troublemakers, not peacemakers. And above all, they were the quintessential persecutors of the righteous. Clearly, the Beatitudes were a rebuke to the Pharisees' whole system.

Jesus deliberately set His description of authentic righteousness against the religion of the Pharisees. The sermon was aimed squarely at them and their unique brand of hypocrisy. Jesus also attacked their method of interpreting Scripture, their means of applying the law, their notions of guilt and merit, their infatuation with ceremonial minutiae, and their love for moral and doctrinal subtleties.

Why did Jesus say again and again in the Sermon on the Mount, "You have heard that it was said to those of old . . . But I say to you . . ." (Matthew 5:21–22)?

The Sermon on the Mount must be understood as Jesus' exposition of Old Testament law, not a different moral standard altogether. He was simply refuting the Pharisees' misconstrued teaching about the law's moral precepts. Jesus was unpacking the true and full meaning of the law as it was originally intended—especially in contrast to the limited, narrow, and woodenly literal approach of the Pharisees. Their hermeneutic (the method by which they interpreted Scripture) led them to expound for hours on the law's invisible fine points while inventing technical twists and turns to make exceptions to some of the law's most important moral precepts.

What is an example of Jesus unpacking the true and full meaning of the law?

Jesus, for instance, raises the issue of the Old Testament's eye-for-an-eye rule (Exodus 21:24–25). This principle was designed to limit penalties assessed in civil and criminal court cases. It was never supposed to authorize private retaliation for petty insults and personal infractions. It was a principle that kept the legal system in check, not a rule designed to unleash neighbor against neighbor in a back-and-forth war of attacks and counter-attacks. But the Pharisees had basically turned it into that. Personal vengeance poisoned the social atmosphere of Israel, and the religious leaders justified it by an appeal to Moses. Jesus said that was a total misuse and abuse of Moses' law.

What exactly did Jesus mean when He closed this section of the Sermon on the Mount with, "You are to be perfect, as your heavenly Father is perfect" (Matthew 5:48 NASB)?

The law itself demands perfection (Leviticus 19:2; 20:26; Deuteronomy 18:13; 27:26; James 2:10). Obviously, Christ set an unattainable standard. Though this standard is impossible for fallen sinners to meet, God could not lower it without compromising His own perfection. He who is perfect could not set an imperfect standard of righteousness. Since no sinner can possibly live up to that standard, we are dependent on grace for salvation. Our own righteousness can never be good enough (Philippians 3:4–9); we desperately need the perfect righteousness of Jesus Christ that God imputes to those who believe (Romans 4:1–8). That is the marvelous truth of the gospel: Christ has met this standard on our behalf.

How did the Pharisees hear Jesus' call to perfection?

The Pharisees believed that their best would be good enough for God—especially if they adorned their religion with as many carefully crafted ceremonies and rituals as possible. That's where all their trust and all their hope for heaven lay. They of course formally recognized that they, too, were imperfect, but they minimized their own imperfections and covered them with public exhibitions of piety. They were convinced that would be good enough for God, mainly because it made them seem so much better than everyone else.

Yet any Pharisee who may have been in the audience for the Sermon on the Mount would have understood Jesus' message plainly enough: Their righteousness, with all its stress on pomp and circumcision, simply did not meet the divine standard. They weren't really any better than the tax collectors. And God would not accept their imperfect righteousness. Jesus was as direct as possible about that.

Did Jesus specifically address the Pharisees' futile practice of their man-made religion?

Practically all of Matthew 6 continues with a hammering, point-by-point critique of the most visible traits of Pharisaism. Jesus was contrasting the religious exhibitionism of the Pharisees with the authentic faith He had described in the Beatitudes. Faith has its primary impact on the heart of the believer. The Pharisees' religion, by contrast, was mainly for show, "to be seen" by others (Matthew 6:1). True saving faith inevitably produces good works, because it expresses itself in love (Galatians 5:6); but the superficial displays of "charity" in works-religion are not even truly charitable. Because Pharisee-style religion is motivated mainly by a craving for the praise of men, it is inherently self-aggrandizing, making it the very antithesis of authentic charity.

In addition to His teaching about the Sabbath, what are some specific practices of the Pharisees that Jesus spoke to?

Jesus rebuked the hypocrisy of *loud, long public prayers* (a specialty of the Pharisees), again saying that the earthly attention such a practice garners is its only reward (Matthew 6:5). At this point He first gave the model prayer that has become known as the Lord's Prayer. That prayer's brevity, simplicity, and Godward focus set it apart from the Pharisees' style of praying.

Jesus also commented on the Pharisees' *fasting.* It was all a charade—a thin veneer that barely covered their totally selfish motives. Legitimate fasting is supposed to help us set aside worldly concerns in order to focus on prayer and spiritual things. The Pharisees instead had turned their fasting into another means of parading their piety in public, proving once more that they could not have cared less about heavenly things. What they really cared for was worldly applause. All their fasting had the exact opposite effect of what a fast should do; it drew attention to them, rather than eliminating things that distract. Jesus exposed the hypocrisy of it.

Why didn't the Pharisees want to change their ways?

All of the Pharisees' animosity toward Jesus was driven by their fear that if He came to power as Messiah, they would lose their status, their means of wealth, and all their earthly advantages (John 11:48). Despite all their pious pretenses, those things meant more to them than righteousness. So when Jesus said, "Seek first the kingdom of God and His righteousness, and all these things shall be added to you" (Matthew 6:33), He was teaching yet another truth that directly assaulted the Pharisees' value system.

What summary of the Old Testament law and teachings did Jesus offer?

Jesus' summary is a single verse, the so-called golden rule: "Whatever you want men to do to you, do also to them, for this is the Law and the Prophets" (Matthew 7:12). The principle of love that defines the golden rule is the underlying principle of all the law. Elsewhere (Matthew 22:36–40), Jesus made it clear that the law demands love for God as well as love for one's neighbors.

What is Jesus' closing point in His Sermon on the Mount?

The final plea of the Sermon on the Mount is a general invitation to "enter by the narrow gate; for wide is the gate and broad is the way that leads to destruction, and there are many who go in by it. Because narrow is the gate and difficult is the way which leads to life, and there are few who find it" (Matthew 7:13–14). The narrow gate and difficult road are references to the gospel's demand for total self-denial and humility—and all the other qualities highlighted in the Beatitudes. Proud and unbroken sinners always choose the wrong road. That's why it is full of travelers. It's broad enough for every-one from out-and-out libertines to the strictest Pharisees. All of them like it, because no one has to bow low or leave any baggage behind in order get on this highway. Furthermore, all the road signs promise heaven. There's just one problem, and it's a significant one: the road does not actually go to heaven. It leads instead to utter destruction.

When Jesus taught, what about His delivery attracted the people's attention?

People "were astonished at His teaching, for He taught them as one having authority, and not as the scribes" (Matthew 7:28–29). The Pharisees could not teach without citing this or that rabbi and resting on the pedigree of centuries-long traditions. Their religion was academic in practically every sense of that word. And to many of them, teaching was just another opportunity to seek praise from men—by showing off their erudition. The Pharisees took great pride in citing as many sources as possible, carefully footnoting their sermons. They were more concerned with what others said about the law than they were with what the law itself actually taught.

Jesus, by contrast, quoted no authority other than the Word of God itself. He gave its interpretation without buttressing His point of view with endless quotations from earlier writers. If Jesus cited religious scholars at all, it was to refute them. He spoke as one who had authority, because He does. He is God, and His style of delivery reflected that. His words were full of love and tenderness toward repentant sinners—but equally full of hard sayings and harsh-sounding words for the self-righteous and self-satisfied. In addition, Jesus wasn't inviting an exchange of opinions, giving an academic lecture, or looking for common cause with the religious leaders of the land; He was declaring the Word of God against them.

What are some truths about God's forgiveness that Jesus taught?

Our God is a forgiving God; that is His nature (Psalm 86:5; Micah 7:18). Jesus emphatically stated that the severity of sin never hinders God's forgiveness: "Every sin and blasphemy" is forgivable (Matthew 12:31). But the language Jesus used ("sin and blasphemy") clearly sets blasphemy apart from all other sins, signifying that any blasphemy is worse than other sins. That's because it is a sin directly against God, with no motive other than dishonoring Him. Blasphemy fulfills no craving, offers no reward, and gratifies no human need. Of all sins, this one is purely and simply an act of defiance against God. That's why in any biblical taxonomy of evil deeds, blasphemy ranks worse than even murder and adultery.

What one unpardonable sin did Jesus teach about?

Jesus spoke of one very specific exhibition of gross blasphemy, and that is what He said was unforgivable. It was the sin of those Pharisees: closing one's heart permanently against Christ even after the Holy Spirit has brought full conviction of the truth.

In effect, Jesus closed the door of heaven against these Pharisees who had so utterly and deliberately shut their hearts against Him. Why did He characterize their sin as blasphemy against the Holy Spirit? Because Jesus' miracles were done in the power of the Holy Spirit. Even the Pharisees knew that in their hearts, yet they claimed He was operating in Satan's power. In effect, they were calling the Holy Spirit the devil and giving the devil credit for what the Spirit of God had done.

What made this particular sin unpardonable was the finality of it. It was deliberate. It was an expression of coldhearted, determined unbelief. These Pharisees had seen, up close, more evidence than they could ever possibly need that Jesus was God incarnate. Their hearts were already settled. They would never believe, no matter what Jesus ever did or said. Therefore their sin was unforgivable.

What harsh words for the Pharisees did Jesus have?

In Matthew 23, Jesus pronounced woe against the Pharisees eight times. Remember that the Sermon on the Mount began with eight beatitudes. These pronouncements of woe are the polar opposite of those, and in stark contrast these are curses rather than blessings. Yet even in the curses, there is a poignancy that reflects Jesus' sorrow. He is not expressing a preference for their condemnation, because, after all, He came to save, not to condemn (John 3:17). God takes no pleasure in the destruction of the wicked (Ezekiel 18:32; 33:11). On the other hand, Jesus' profound sorrow over the hardhearted rebellion of the Pharisees did not move Him to soften His words or soft-sell the reality of the spiritual calamity they had brought upon themselves. If anything, that was why He delivered this final message to them with such passion and urgency.

Jesus began seven of the eight woes with, "Woe to you, scribes and Pharisees, hypocrites!" What is significant about His calling the Pharisees hypocrites?

In pronouncing the eight woes, Jesus addressed many of the doctrinal and practical errors that illustrated what deplorable hypocrites the Pharisees were. These included their pretentious praying (Matthew 23:14); their misguided motives for "ministry" to others (Matthew 23:15); their tendency to swear casually by things that are holy, plus the corresponding habit of playing fast and loose with their vows (Matthew 23:18–22); their upside-down approach to priorities, by which they had elevated obscure ceremonial precepts over the moral law (Matthew 23:23–24); and above all, their blithe toleration of many gross, often ludicrous, manifestations of hypocrisy (Matthew 23:27–31).

What other aspect of Jesus' teaching here offended the religious establishment?

One other characteristic that makes this sermon stand out is Jesus' liberal use of derogatory epithets. Those who think name-calling is inherently un-Christlike and always inappropriate will have a very hard time with this sermon. In addition to the eight times Jesus emphatically calls them "hypocrites!" He calls them "blind guides" (Matthew 23:16, 24); "fools and blind!" (Matthew 23:17, 19); "blind Pharisee[s]" (Matthew 23:26); and "serpents, brood of vipers!" (Matthew 23:33).

What did Jesus mean when He called His followers to "take his cross and follow after Me" (Matthew 10:38)?

This is Jesus' first mention of the word *cross* to His disciples. To them it would have evoked a picture of a violent, degrading death. He was demanding total commitment from them—even unto physical death—and making this call to full surrender a part of the message they were to proclaim to others. Those who come to Christ with self-renouncing faith receive true and eternal life.

What was significant about Jesus' encounter with the woman at the well (see John 4)?

For a Jewish man to speak to a woman in public, let alone to ask from her, a Samaritan, a drink, was a definite breach of rigid social custom as well as a marked departure from the social animosity that existed between the two groups. Further, a "rabbi" and religious leader did not hold conversations with women of ill repute (John 4:18)

Jesus went on to use the woman's need for physical water to sustain life in that arid region in order to serve as an object lesson for her need for spiritual transformation. The woman did not realize that Jesus was talking about her spiritual needs. Instead, she wanted such water in order to avoid her frequent trips to the well.

What truth did Jesus set forth clearly for the woman at the well and also for His followers today?

In John 4:24, Jesus clearly stated, "God is Spirit," the classical statement on the nature of God. The phrase means that God is invisible as opposed to the physical or material nature of man. Man could never comprehend the invisible God unless He revealed Himself, as He did in Scripture and the incarnation. Jesus also taught that a person must worship not simply by external conformity to religious rituals and places (outwardly), but inwardly (in spirit) with the proper heart attitude.

In John 4:26, Jesus also forthrightly declared Himself to be Messiah, though His habit was to avoid such declarations to His own Jewish people who had such crassly political and militaristic views regarding Messiah.

What did Jesus mean when He told Nicodemus—a Jewish leader, a Pharisee, and a member of the Sanhedrin—that he needed to be born again?

Jesus chose the perfect language to convey to Nicodemus that true righteousness comes not from one's works but through faith in Christ: "Unless one is born again, he cannot see the kingdom of God" (John 3:3). With that simple statement, Jesus demolished Nicodemus's entire worldview: his Jewish birth and upbringing; his attainments as a leading Pharisee; the care with which he kept himself from ceremonial defilement; the respect he had earned in the eyes of his countrymen; the merit he thought he had stored up for himself. Whatever else Jesus meant, this much was plain: Jesus was demanding that Nicodemus forsake everything he stood for, walk away from everything he had ever done as a Pharisee, abandon hope in everything he ever trusted, and start all over from the beginning.

In response, Nicodemus said, "How can a man be born when he is old? Can he enter a second time into his mother's womb and be born?" (John 3:4). Did Nicodemus really not understand what Jesus meant?

Don't imagine that Nicodemus was so naive as to think Jesus was telling him he literally needed to be physically reborn. Nicodemus must have been a highly skilled teacher himself, or he would not have attained his position. His question to Jesus should no more be interpreted as a literal reference to physical birth than Jesus' original remark to him. His rejoinder to Jesus merely picked up on Jesus' imagery.

What did Nicodemus probably understand Jesus to be saying?

Jesus was telling Nicodemus, in language Nicodemus was sure to grasp, that not only was He not speaking of any superficial or fleshly self-reformation, but He was in fact calling for something Nicodemus was powerless to do for himself. This punctured the heart of Nicodemus's religious convictions. To a Pharisee like him, the worst imaginable news would be that there was nothing he could possibly do to help himself spiritually. Jesus had described Nicodemus's case as utterly hopeless. Talk about harsh! But that is, after all, the very starting point of the gospel message. Sinners are "dead in trespasses and sins . . . by nature children of wrath . . . having no hope and without God" (Ephesians 2:1, 3, 12).

Why was Jesus so harsh with Nicodemus?

Jesus was not being mean-spirited, but precisely the opposite. Nicodemus needed to recognize his spiritual poverty and see his need for a Savior. And Jesus cared more for the truth than He cared about how Nicodemus felt about it. Sometimes the truth isn't "nice"—but it's always focused and unyielding. Before Nicodemus could receive any help from Jesus, he needed to see how desperate his situation was. When a patient has a life-threatening illness that urgently needs treatment, the physician needs to give him the bad news candidly. That was the case with Nicodemus.

What can today's defenders of the faith learn from Jesus?

Jesus knew something Christians today often forget: truth doesn't defeat error by waging a public relations campaign. The struggle between truth and error is spiritual warfare (Ephesians 6:12), and truth has no way to defeat falsehood except by exposing and refuting lies and false teaching. That calls for candor and clarity, boldness, and precision—and sometimes more severity than congeniality.

Parables

In addition to His more direct teaching, Jesus also taught in parables. He told thirty-nine parables: most in Matthew and Luke, a small number in Mark, and none in John.

What is a parable?

A common form of teaching in Judaism, a parable is a long analogy, often cast in the form of a story. At the beginning of His ministry, Jesus had used many graphic analogies, but their meaning was fairly clear in the context of His teaching. Parables require more explanation, and Jesus used them to obscure the truth from unbelievers while making it clearer to His disciples. For the remainder of His Galilean ministry, in fact, He did not speak to the multitudes except in parables (Matthew 13:34).

Why did Jesus choose to teach
in a way that was not readily
understood by all His hearers?

In Matthew 13:11, Jesus clearly affirmed that
the ability to comprehend spiritual truth is a
gracious gift of God bestowed by the sovereign
God. Jesus then explained, "I speak to [the reprobate people] in parables, because seeing they do
not see, and hearing they do not hear, nor do they
understand" (Matthew 13:13). Jesus' veiling the
truth from unbelievers this way was both an act of
judgment and an act of mercy: judgment because
it kept them in the darkness they loved; but mercy
because they had already rejected the light, so any
exposure to more truth would only increase their
condemnation.

What are some of the parables Jesus told that both puzzled and enlightened—and what truths did they teach?

The Camel and the Eye of Needle

> "It is easier for a camel to go through the eye of a needle than for a rich man to enter the kingdom of God." (Mark 10:25)

The Persians expressed impossibility by saying it would be easier to put an elephant through the eye of a needle. This was a Jewish colloquially adaptation of that expression denoting impossibility (the largest animal in Palestine was a camel). Jesus used this illustration to say explicitly that salvation by human effort is impossible; it is wholly by God's grace. The Jews believed that with alms a person purchased salvation, so the more wealth one had, the more alms he could give, the more sacrifices and offerings he could offer, thus purchasing redemption. Jesus taught that not even the rich could buy salvation. Salvation is entirely a gracious, sovereign work of God.

The Wheat and Tares

"The kingdom of heaven is like a man who sowed good seed in his field; but while men slept, his enemy came and sowed tares among the wheat and went his way. But when the grain had sprouted and produced a crop, then the tares also appeared. So the servants of the owner came and said to him, 'Sir, did you not sow good seed in your field? How then does it have tares?' He said to them, 'An enemy has done this.' The servants said to him, 'Do you want us then to go and gather them up?' But he said, 'No, lest while you gather up the tares you also uproot the wheat with them. Let both grow together until the harvest, and at the time of harvest I will say to the reapers, "First gather together the tares and bind them in bundles to burn them, but gather the wheat into my barn."'" (Matthew 13:24–30)

In an agricultural setting, sowing darnel in someone else's wheat field was a way for enemies to destroy someone's livelihood catastrophically. Here it pictures Satan's efforts to deceive the church by mingling his children with God's, in some cases making it impossible for believers to discern the true from the false.

The Mustard Seed and the Leaven

> "The kingdom of heaven is like a mustard seed, which a man took and sowed in his field, which indeed is the least of all the seeds; but when it is grown it is greater than the herbs and becomes a tree, so that the birds of the air come and nest in its branches. . . . The kingdom of heaven is like leaven, which a woman took and hid in three measures of meal till it was all leavened." (Matthew 13:31–33)

In teaching about the kingdom of heaven, Jesus compared it to Palestinian mustard plants, large shrubs, sometimes up to fifteen feet high, that were certainly big enough for birds to lodge in. The kingdom is also pictured as yeast, multiplying quietly and permeating all that it contacts. Jesus repeatedly described the kingdom as the pervading influence.

The Prodigal Son

> "When [the son] was still a great way off, his father saw him and had compassion, and ran and fell on his neck and kissed him." (Luke 15:20)

The father's response to his son, returning home after a season of wanton immorality and wasteful extravagance with his father's wealth, illustrates God's love toward a penitent sinner and the power of confession. Even while the profligate boy is still a long way off, the father sees him (which means the father must have been looking for his wayward son). He "ran and embraced him and kissed him" (Luke 15:20 NASB). The verb tense indicates that the father kissed the son over and over. Here is tender mercy. Here is forgiveness. Here is compassion.

Here is a father treating the son as if there were no past, as if his sins had been buried in the depths of the deepest sea, removed as far as the east is from the west, and forgotten. Here is unrestrained affection, unconditional love. The father's response is remarkable. There is no diffidence. There is no hesitation. There is no withholding of emotion, no subtle coolness. There is only sympathetic, eager, pure, unbridled love. The father loves his wayward child lavishly. He loves him profusely. He loves him grandly.

In this parable, the most familiar and beloved of all that Christ told, we are to learn that God's love is like the love of this father. It is not minimal; it is unreserved. It is unrestrained. It is extravagant. It is not bestowed in moderation. There is no holding back—just pure love undiluted, without any resentment or disaffection. The father receives the wayward boy as a privileged son, not as a lowly servant.

Above all, the love of the father was an unconditional love. It was undiminished by the rebellion of the son. Despite all that this boy had done to deserve his father's wrath, the father responded with unrestrained love. Though the young man may not have realized it while he was languishing in the far country, he could not be estranged from so loving a father. Even his great sins could not ultimately separate him from his father's love. Similarly, our Father wants us to return and to confess—He waits with open arms.

The Wicked Vinedressers

> "Still having one son, his beloved, [the owner of the vineyard] also sent him to them last, saying, 'They will respect my son.' But those vinedressers said among themselves, 'This is the heir. Come, let us kill him, and the inheritance will be ours.'" (Mark 12:6–7; also Matthew 21:33–46 and Luke 20:9–19)

In Scripture, the vineyard is a common symbol for the Jewish nation. Here the landowner, representing God, develops the vineyard with great care, then leases it to vinedressers, representing the Jewish leaders. (Luke alone noted the parable was addressed to all the people, not just the Jewish leaders.) In Mark's account, three different servants came individually. The tenants "beat" the first one, "threw stones at" the second, and "killed" the third. The vinedresser's son ("beloved son" in Mark and Luke) represents the Lord Jesus Christ. The greedy vinedressers wanted the entire harvest and the vineyard for themselves. They would stop at nothing to achieve that end, so they plotted to kill the owner's son. This behavior corresponds to the Jewish rulers' treatment of many of the Old Testament prophets. The chief priests, scribes, and elders were aware that Christ was condemning their actions, but it aroused their hatred, not their repentance.

The Good Samaritan

> "So which of these three do you think was neighbor to him who fell among the thieves?" And [the lawyer who was testing Jesus] said, "He who showed mercy on him." Then Jesus said to him, "Go and do likewise." (Luke 10:36–37)

The prevailing opinion among scribes and Pharisees was that one's neighbors were the righteous alone. According to these religious leaders, the wicked—including rank sinners (such as tax collectors and prostitutes), Gentiles, and especially Samaritans—were to be hated because they were the enemies of God. But the truly righteous person's "hatred" for sinners is marked by a broken-hearted grieving over the condition of the sinner. And as Jesus taught, it is also tempered by a genuine love. The Pharisees had elevated hostility toward the wicked to the status of a virtue, in effect nullifying the second Great Commandment to love their neighbors (Matthew 22:39). Jesus' answer to this lawyer demolished that pharisaical excuse for hating one's enemies.

Additional Teachings

What are some of the truths Jesus taught without using a parable?

The Foundation for a House

> "Whoever hears these sayings of Mine, and does them, I will liken him to a wise man who built his house on the rock: and the rain descended, the floods came, and the winds blew and beat on that house; and it did not fall, for it was founded on the rock." (Matthew 7:24–25)

The house represents a religious life; the rain represents divine judgment. Only the one built on the foundation of obedience to God's Word stands.

This obedience calls for repentance, rejection of salvation by works, and trust in God's grace to save through His merciful provision.

The Rich Young Ruler

> "Good Teacher, what good thing shall I do that I may have eternal life?" So [Jesus] said to him, "Why do you call Me good? No one is good but One, that is, God." (Matthew 19:16–17)

Jesus was not disclaiming His own deity but rather teaching the young man that all but God are sinners. This young man's most serious spiritual defect was his reluctance to confess his own utter spiritual bankruptcy.

> "If you want to enter into life, keep the commandments." (Matthew 19:17)

This teaching, of course, is law, not gospel. Before showing him the way to life, Jesus impressed on the young man both the high standard required by God and the absolute futility of seeking salvation by his own merit. The young man should have responded as the disciples did (Matthew 19:25) and confessed that keeping the law perfectly is impossible, but instead the young man confidently declared that he qualified for heaven under those terms: "All these things I have kept from my youth" (Matthew 19:20). The self-righteous young man would not admit his own sin.

"Go, sell what you have and give to the poor." (Matthew 19:21)

Jesus was not setting forth terms for salvation but exposing the young man's true heart. His refusal to obey here reveals two things: (1) he was not blameless as far as the law was concerned because he was guilty of loving himself and his possessions more than his neighbors; and (2) he lacked true faith, which involves a willingness to surrender all at Christ's bidding. Jesus was not teaching salvation by philanthropy, but He was demanding that this young man give Him first place. The young man failed the test. Because his own love of his possessions was such a stumbling block, he had already rejected Jesus' claim to lordship over his life.

Who Is the Greatest in the Kingdom of Heaven?

"Unless you are converted and become as little children, you will by no means enter the kingdom of heaven." (Matthew 18:3)

"Become as little children" is how Jesus characterized conversion. Like the Beatitudes, this verse pictures faith as the simple, helpless, trusting dependence of those who have no resources of their own. Like children, they have no achievements and no accomplishments to offer or with which to commend themselves.

Count the Cost of Discipleship

"If anyone comes to Me and does not hate his father and mother, wife and children, brothers and sisters, yes, and his own life also, he cannot be My disciple. And whoever does not bear his cross and come after Me cannot be My disciple." (Luke 14:26–27)

Christ's aim was not to gather appreciative crowds, but to make true disciples. He never adapted His message to majority preferences, but always plainly declared the high cost of discipleship. Here, He made several bold demands that would discourage the halfhearted. He was demanding total commitment from them—even unto physical death—and making this call to full surrender a part of the message they were to proclaim to others. The "hatred" called for here is actually a lesser love. Jesus was calling His disciples to cultivate such a devotion to Him that their attachment to everything else—including their own lives—would seem like hatred by comparison. The multitudes Jesus taught were positive but uncommitted. Far from making it easy for them to accept His teaching, He set the cost of discipleship as high as possible—and encouraged them to do a careful inventory before declaring their willingness to follow. Christ continually emphasized the difficulty of following Him: Salvation is by grace alone, but it is not easy. It calls for knowledge of the truth, repentance, submission to Christ as Lord, and a willingness to obey His will and Word.

Servant Leadership

> "Whoever desires to become great among you, let him be your servant. And whoever desires to be first among you, let him be your slave." (Matthew 20:26–27)

Jesus was the supreme example of servant leadership. The King of kings and Lord of lords relinquished His privileges and gave His life as a selfless sacrifice in serving others. Christ's substitutionary death on behalf of those who would put their faith in Him is the most glorious, blessed truth in all of Scripture. The ransom price was paid to God to satisfy His justice and holy wrath against sin. In paying it, Christ "bore our sins in His own body on the [cross]" (1 Peter 2:24).

Reactions to Jesus' Teachings

Why didn't the religious leaders of His day accept Jesus?

Misconstrue the gospel or adapt it to suit a particular subculture's preferences, and the inevitable result will be a religion of works and a system that breeds self-righteousness. That is exactly what Jesus' conflict with the Pharisees was all about. They represented a style of religion and a system of belief that was in direct conflict with the very heart of the gospel He proclaimed. Jesus, for instance, offered forgiveness and instant justification to believing sinners. Israel's religious leaders manufactured massive systems of works and ceremonies that in effect made justification itself a human work. In the words of the apostle Paul, "they [were] ignorant of God's righteousness, and seeking to establish their own righteousness" (Romans 10:3). There was simply no way for Christ to avoid conflict with these leaders. So instead, He made the most of it. He used their false religion as a foil for the truth He taught.

Why were religious people of the day upset when Jesus dined with tax collectors and sinners?

That a rabbi would be willing to fraternize at a party with such people was utterly repugnant to the Pharisees. It was diametrically opposed to all their doctrines about separation and ceremonial uncleanness. Here was yet another pet issue of the Pharisees, and Jesus was openly violating their standards, knowing full well that they were watching him closely. From their perspective, it must have seemed as if He was deliberately flaunting His contempt for their system. Because He was.

Why were the religious leaders so passionate about getting rid of Jesus?

It was absolutely clear to the multitudes that Jesus spoke for God, because there was no miracle He could not accomplish, no ailment He could not heal, and no argument from the Jewish leaders He could not answer.

And Israel's religious elite were desperate: "What shall we do? For this Man works many signs. If we let Him alone like this, everyone will believe in Him, and the Romans will come and take away both our place and nation" (John 11:47–48). Notice that they did not dispute the legitimacy of Jesus' claim that He was the Messiah or the reality of His miracles. They had no real argument against His doctrine, either—other than the fact that He represented a serious threat to their power.

In short, the chief priests and Pharisees feared the Romans more than they feared God. They wanted to hang on to the clout they had, rather than yield their honor and obedience to Israel's rightful Messiah. They loved their own artificial piety more than they craved authentic righteousness. They were satisfied with their own merits and contemptuous of anyone who questioned their godliness—as Jesus had done publicly and repeatedly. From the time He first entered public ministry, He had stood resolutely against their whole system of religion, and they hated Him for it.

When did Jesus clearly declare with His words rather than just His miracles that He was Son of God?

For Jesus to call God "My Father" (especially in a context where He was likening Himself to God) was to suggest that He was of the same essence as God the Father—thus "making Himself equal with God" (John 5:18). Jesus first used that expression publicly when He was twelve years old, when He said to His parents, "Did you not know that I must be about My Father's business?" (Luke 2:49). The second time Jesus spoke these words was when He first cleansed the Temple, saying, "Do not make My Father's house a house of merchandise!" (John 2:16). After this, He frequently spoke of God as "My Father." When the Jews learned that Jesus had healed a man on the Sabbath, Jesus responded with, in effect, an explicit and public unveiling of the truth that He was God's only-begotten Son; that He was not just a prophet or brilliant rabbi, but fully God incarnate. As soon as He used that expression here, all hell broke loose against Him. The majority of Israel's religious leaders, already His sworn enemies, "sought all the more to kill Him" (John 5:18).

Why did Jesus treat His opponents so harshly?

If the stridency of Jesus' dealings with the Jewish leaders shocks you, bear in mind that He had the advantage of knowing their hearts even more perfectly than they themselves did.

Also realize that Jesus was not trying to provoke them merely for sport. He had a gracious reason for using the kind of harsh speech many today would unthinkingly label ungracious: "I say these things that you may be saved" (John 5:34). The religious leaders of Israel were lost and progressively hardening their hearts against Jesus. They needed some harsh words. Jesus would not permit them to ignore Him, or to ignore His truth, under the guise of showing them the kind of deference and public honor they craved from Him.

Furthermore, Jesus' constant friction with the Pharisees does show that conflict is sometimes necessary. Harsh words are not always inappropriate.

Unpleasant and unwelcome truths sometimes need to be voiced. False religion always needs to be answered. Love may cover a multitude of sins (1 Peter 4:8), but the gross hypocrisy of false teachers desperately needs to be uncovered—lest our silence facilitate and perpetuate a damning delusion. The truth is not always "nice."

Didn't Jesus care about how people felt when He taught?

The truth mattered more to Jesus than how people felt about it or Him. He wasn't looking for ways just to make people like Him; He was calling people who were willing to bow to Him unconditionally as their Lord. He wasn't interested in reinforcing the common-ground beliefs where His message overlapped with the Pharisees' worldview. On the contrary, Jesus stressed (almost exclusively) the points on which He disagreed with them. He never acted as if the best way to turn people away from the damnable heresies of Pharisee-religion was to make His message sound as much as possible like the popular beliefs of the day. Instead, He stressed (and reiterated again and again) the points of doctrine that were most at odds with the conventional wisdom of Pharisaism.

When Jesus discussed the Pharisees' approach to their religious life, He seemed to be commenting on more than, say, hand washing or observing the Sabbath. What was the real issue?

The bigger, underlying issue in the Pharisees' dialogue with Jesus about cleansing or washing or anything was the principle of justification and how sinners can be made right with God. Justification is not earned by merit, nor is it gained through rituals. True righteousness cannot be earned by human works; forgiveness and full justification are freely given to those who believe.

In other words, the difference between Jesus and the Pharisees was not that they had differing customs regarding how to observe the Sabbath; it was that they held contradictory views on the way of salvation. That truth was too important to bury under the blanket of an artificial civility. The gospel must be defended against lies and false teaching, and the fact that gospel truth often offends even the most distinguished religious people is never a reason for trying to tame the message or tone it down. Jesus Himself modeled that.

So, then, what was the main purpose of Jesus' teaching and preaching?

Jesus was not interested in increasing the ranks of halfhearted disciples. His preaching had one aim: to declare truth, not to win accolades from the audience. For those who were not interested in hearing the truth, He did not try to make it easier to receive. What He did instead was make it impossible to ignore.

By the way, the contemporary craving for shallow sermons that please and entertain is at least partly rooted in the popular myth that Jesus Himself was always likable, agreeable, winsome, and at the cutting edge of His culture's fashions. As we have seen, even a cursory look at Jesus' preaching ministry reveals a totally different picture. Jesus' sermons usually featured hard truths, harsh words, and high-octane controversy. His own disciples complained that His preaching was too hard to hear (John 6:60)! Again, Jesus' preaching heads the list of things that make Him impossible to ignore.

Jesus: His Passion

Jesus Christ was the only truly sinless individual who ever lived—the most virtuous man of all time. He "committed no sin, nor was deceit found in His mouth" (1 Peter 2:22). He was "holy, harmless, undefiled, separate from sinners" (Hebrews 7:26). And yet the torment and punishment He suffered in His death was infinitely more heinous than anyone else has ever suffered. He bore the full weight of retribution for human evil. He suffered as if He were guilty of humanity's worst offenses. And yet He was guilty of nothing.

Palm Sunday

Jesus entered Jerusalem to celebrate the Passover and, as the Lamb of God, consummate His ministry by dying on behalf of sinful human beings. What evidence in the Mark 11:1–11 description is there that the people were welcoming Him as military leader and king?

Jesus' Palm Sunday entry into Jerusalem is traditionally called His triumphal entry, but more accurately, it was His coronation as the true King. Jesus entered the city on a young donkey: at that time the Jews regarded animals that had never been ridden as especially suited for holy purposes.

The people alongside the road spread their clothes, part of the ancient practice of welcoming a new king. The palm branches they waved symbolized joy and salvation. The crowd was excited and filled with praise for the Messiah who taught with such authority, healed the sick, and raised Lazarus from the dead. The people's cry of "Hosanna!" was originally a Hebrew prayer meaning "save now."

The festive Palm Sunday scene when Jesus entered Jerusalem offered no hints as to what the week held for the one the crowd hailed with "Hosanna!" Why were the people so excited?

It looked for all the world as if Jesus would be swept on a massive wave of public support into prominence and power in some political capacity—and then He would finally inaugurate His promised kingdom. But the public's enthusiasm for Christ was an illusion. Their expectation was for a Messiah who would quickly liberate Israel from the dominion of Rome and establish a political kingdom that would ultimately rule over even Caesar. Jerusalem was happy to have a worker of miracles and the hope of a conquering King like that. But they did not want Jesus' hard preaching. They were shocked that He seemed more interested in challenging their religious institutions than

He was in conquering Rome and liberating them from political oppression. They were stunned by His treatment of Israel's religious elite—as if they were pagans. He spent more time calling Israel to repentance than He did criticizing her oppressors. On top of that, they did not appreciate His refusal to be Messiah on their terms (John 6:15). Before the week was over, the same crowd who praised Him with "Hosanna!" would be screaming for His blood.

Cleansing
the Temple

Now in Jerusalem, Jesus went to
the temple and cleansed it just as
He had done three years earlier.
Why was this act significant?

The temple had become more corrupt and profane than ever. Animals to be used as sacrifices—that were sure to pass the high priest's inspection—were for sale. Greek and Roman coins were exchanged for Jewish or Tyrian coins, which every Jewish male twenty and older had to use for the annual half-shekel payment for temple religious services. A fee as high as ten or twelve percent was assessed for this exchange service. And the temple court was being used as a shortcut through which to carry merchandise to other parts of Jerusalem. All of these activities revealed irreverence for the temple—and ultimately for God Himself. The temple had become a place where God's people, instead of being able to worship undisturbed, were extorted, and their extortioners were protected. With this temple cleansing, Jesus showed vividly that He was on a divine mission as the Son of God.

The Last Supper

Based on the history of the Passover, what is significant about this particular celebration of the historic event?

Faithful Jews celebrated Passover with the sacrifice of a spotless lamb to commemorate their nation's deliverance from slavery in Egypt. At the first Passover, the people of Israel sacrificed a perfect lamb and spread its blood on the door frame of the home. At God's command, the angel of death killed the firstborn of every Egyptian family, but he passed over the Israelite homes where the doorposts were covered by the blood of a lamb.

According to God's sovereign plans, this important Jewish celebration dovetailed with the

Jewish leaders' desire to kill Jesus. These leaders were fearful that Christ's popularity among the people would result in pressure to recognize Him as the rightful ruler of the Jews—Messiah. Such a move would disrupt their uneasy peace with Rome. That in turn would pose a threat to the status of the high priest and Sanhedrin. The Jewish leaders were therefore doing all they could to quell the messianic fervor sweeping through Israel. They decided they had to silence Jesus quickly, whether He was the true Messiah or not. But Passover was God's time—the time He had chosen, the time most fitting for the Lamb of God to die for the sins of the world.

When Jesus and His disciples gathered for the Passover meal, why did Jesus wash everyone's feet?

Foot washing was a task typically delegated to the lowest slave. It removed the dust, mud, and other filth encountered on the unpaved roads in and around Jerusalem. Evidently there was no servant to perform the task when Jesus and the disciples arrived. Instead of humbling themselves to perform such a demeaning task for one another, the disciples had simply left their feet unwashed. Taking the role of the lowest servant, Christ transformed the washing into an object lesson about humility and true holiness (John 13:6–9).

In what ways did the Last Supper point to the church's celebration of communion?

The unleavened bread eaten at Passover symbolized the severing of the Israelites from the old life in Egypt. It represented a separation from worldliness, sin, and false religion and the beginning of a new life of holiness and godliness. From then on, in the Lord's Supper, the bread would symbolize Christ's body, which He sacrificed for the salvation of humankind, for our deliverance from sin and our new birth. The shedding of blood in a sacrifice was always God's requirement in establishing any covenant. The shedding of blood had also protected the Jewish people from death at the original Passover. Here, Christ's blood needed to be shed for the remission of sins, a protection from permanent separation from God, eternal death.

Jesus' Prayers at Gethsemane

When Jesus prayed in Gethsemane and asked if God would "take this cup away" (Luke 22:42), what exactly was Jesus referring to?

T he cup" was not merely death. It was not the physical pain of the cross. It was not the scourging or the humiliation. It was not the horrible thirst, the torture of having nails driven through His body, or the disgrace of being spat upon or beaten. It was not even all those things combined. All of those were the very things Christ Himself had said *not* to fear (Luke 12:4). What

Christ dreaded most about the cross—the cup from which He asked to be delivered if possible—was the outpouring of divine wrath He would have to endure from His holy Father.

So when Christ prayed that if possible the cup might pass from Him, He spoke of drinking the cup of divine judgment. Do not imagine for a moment that Christ feared the earthly pain of crucifixion. He would not have trembled at the prospect of what men could do to Him. There was not one ounce of the fear of man in Him. But He was to "bear the sins of many" (Hebrews 9:28)—and the fullness of divine wrath would fall on Him. In some mysterious way that our human minds could never fathom, God the Father would turn His face from Christ the Son, and Christ would bear the full brunt of the divine fury against sin.

Jesus must have realized that there was no way the cup could pass from Him, so why did He pray like this in the garden?

The plan of salvation was determined by God long ago, before the world was created. In keeping with that eternal plan, God the Son agreed to become a man and die to pay the penalty for sin. So of course Jesus knew that the cup of death and separation from God would not pass from Him. But His "Take this cup" prayer was an honest expression of human passion, of the dread He was feeling at the moment. He was not actually hoping to be released from the role of sin-bearer, and that is made clear by the remainder of His prayer: "Nevertheless, not as I will, but as You will" (Matthew 26:39). Notice the second time Jesus prayed: "O My Father, if this cup cannot pass away from Me unless I drink it, Your will be done" (Matthew 26:42). As the intensity of the agony increases, so does the sense of Jesus' determination to do the will of His Father. What is revealed in the prayer is Jesus' complete surrender of those human passions to the divine will.

Again, what motivates Christ's praying here is not a sinful weakness but normal human infirmity—no different from His hunger, thirst, or fatigue. Christ certainly had no masochistic love of suffering. There would be something inhuman about Him if He did not look forward to the cross with a deep uneasiness and dread of what was to come. But this is not a craven fear; it is the same horror and foreboding any of us would feel if we knew we were about to undergo something extremely painful. In Jesus' case, however, the agony was infinitely magnified because of the nature of what He faced.

The Arrest

Why did so many people go to Gethsemane to arrest Jesus?

None of the gospels gives a numerical estimate of the size of the mob, but Matthew, Mark, and Luke all agree that it was a great multitude (Matthew 26:47; Mark 14:43; Luke 22:47). Depending on the size of the detachment of soldiers (there were six hundred soldiers in a typical Roman cohort), the crowd could easily have numbered in the hundreds. The fact that the chief priests sent such a large crowd to make the arrest indicates the degree to which they were frightened of Jesus' power. Many times before this they had sought to arrest Him or silence Him, and their schemes had always been foiled. Jesus Himself called attention to their absurd and cowardly tactic of sending an armed multitude to arrest Him in the middle of the night. Such a large group was clearly overkill—and it was also unnecessary. They would face no resistance from Jesus. If He had *not* been willing to be arrested, no amount of earthly force would have been sufficient to capture Him. If it were not now His time in the perfect plan of God, He could easily have escaped even from such a large mob, as Jesus pointed out to Peter (Matthew 26:53).

How did the mob know which man in the garden was Jesus?

Judas was the disciple who betrayed Jesus, and Judas had told the soldiers, "Whomever I kiss, He is the One; seize Him" (Matthew 26:48). The kiss in that culture was a sign of respect and homage as well as affection. Slaves kissed the feet of their masters as the utmost sign of respect. Disciples sometimes kissed the hem of their teacher's garment as a token of reverence and deep devotion. It was common to kiss someone on the hand as a gesture of respect and honor. But a kiss on the face, especially with an embrace, signified personal friendship and affection. As if it weren't enough for Judas to betray Jesus, in doing so he pretended the utmost affection, making his act even more despicable.

The arrest was easy, and it was time to move to the trial. What difficulty did Jesus' accusers encounter?

Finding witnesses to testify against this innocent man was not easy. Many people who were willing to bear false witness against Jesus came forward, but none were found credible enough to sustain a charge against Him. Finally two false witnesses came forward. There were obvious discrepancies in the stories told by the witnesses, so their testimony should have been automatically disallowed and the case against Jesus dismissed. But the Sanhedrin was obviously in no mood for that.

Instead, there were enough similarities in what the false witnesses said to give their testimony a veneer of credibility. And the testimony could be twisted to suggest that Jesus was advocating the total overthrow of the Jewish religion (by replacing the current temple with another). Furthermore, the Sanhedrin could charge Him with high blasphemy for claiming that He could rebuild the temple—under construction for forty-six years (John 2:20)—by miraculous means ("without hands" in Mark 14:58).

The Trials

Did the Sanhedrin treat Jesus fairly?

No. The Sanhedrin—the highest court in Israel—rushed Jesus through a kangaroo court into a guilty verdict that had been arranged and agreed upon beforehand. In fact, instead of ruling justly, the Sanhedrin was often motivated by political ambition, greed, and selfishness in its decisions. Consider the traditions and safeguards of justice they violated in Jesus' case: A full day of fasting had to be observed by the council between the passing of sentence and the execution of the criminal. The council could only try cases where an outside party had brought the charges. If charges had been brought against the accused by council members, the entire council was disqualified from trying the case. The testimony of all witnesses had to be precise as to the date, time, and location of the event one was testifying about. The accused was to be presumed innocent until an official guilty verdict was reached. And criminal trials were not to be convened at night.

Why did Jesus never say anything in His defense?

As the defendant, Jesus had no obligation to testify against Himself. So when He stood before Annas and later Caiaphas, He made that point in a dramatic way—by simply declining to testify against Himself. At least seven hundred years earlier, the prophet Isaiah had foretold that very silence: "He was oppressed and He was afflicted, yet He opened not His mouth; He was led as a lamb to the slaughter, and as a sheep before its shearers is silent, so He opened not His mouth" (Isaiah 53:7).

As these bogus trials were playing themselves out, Peter denied ever knowing Jesus. Why did Peter fall?

Peter's failure did not occur spontaneously. Peter himself took the wrong steps that put him on the pathway to failure. Put simply, *Peter boasted too loudly*. He frequently spoke before he thought, and he apparently had no trouble arguing with Jesus. Peter kept on insisting that he would never fall away, and his braggadocio proved his folly, not his faithfulness. Peter also erred because *he prayed too little*. Prayer was the one thing that could have strengthened Peter to face the temptation Jesus had warned him about. Third, *Peter slept too much*. Peter was probably still trying to shake off his sleepy stupor when he impulsively drew his sword and struck the high priest's servant. Peter also *followed from too far*. After fleeing from the garden, Peter followed Christ from a distance. Like many followers today, Peter tried to avoid public identification as a Christian, so he found himself acting like a non-Christian.

Was there a key moment in these bogus trials that clinched Jesus' death?

That moment came when the Sanhedrin asked Jesus, "Are You then the Son of God?" This time He replied simply, "You rightly say that I am" (Luke 22:70). This statement was exactly what they wanted. Now they had Him on record, in broad daylight, claiming by clear implication to be the Son of God. Though Jesus had given ample evidence throughout His ministry to substantiate the claim—some of these men had even seen that evidence with their own eyes—the members of the Sanhedrin were not the least bit interested in either establishing or disproving the validity of Jesus' claim. All they wanted to do now was get Him on the cross as quickly as possible. In the end, it meant they crucified Him for telling the truth.

Jesus Before Pilate

Once the Sanhedrin found Jesus guilty of blasphemy, why did this Jewish rabbi have to go to trial before the Roman authorities, namely Pilate?

Jesus had two trials, one Jewish and religious, the other Roman and secular. Rome reserved the right of execution in capital cases, so Jesus had to be handed over to the Roman authorities for execution. The Sanhedrin took Christ before Pilate. Jesus was then sent to Herod for yet another hearing (Luke 23:6–12) and then returned to Pilate for the final hearing and the sentencing (Luke 23:15–26).

Pilate was willing to let Jesus go free. Why did the crowd object?

It was clear that the bloodthirsty crowd would be satisfied with nothing less than the destruction of Jesus. It mattered nothing to them that no legitimate charges had been brought against Him. They cared little about truth or justice. They wanted a crucifixion. Many in the crowd were blindly following the lead of the Sanhedrin, but there were undoubtedly many others who hated Jesus for all the same reasons people today hate Him: His teaching confronted their wicked lifestyles; His demands were too hard; the truth He taught was too narrow for their tastes. The real issue, in every case, was that "men loved darkness rather than light, because their deeds were evil" (John 3:19).

Pilate ordered Jesus to be flogged
before being nailed to a cross.
What did a flogging involve?

Scourging alone was sometimes fatal. A Roman
scourge was a short wooden handle with
numerous long lashes of leather attached to it.
Each leather strip had a sharp piece of glass, metal,
bone, or other hard object attached to the end of
it. The victim would be stripped of all clothing and
tied to a post by his wrists with his hands high
enough over his head to virtually lift him off the
ground. The feet would be dangling, and the skin
on the back and buttocks completely taut. One or
two scourge-bearers (lictors) would then deliver
blows, skillfully laying the lashes diagonally across
the back and buttocks with extreme force. The skin
would literally be torn away, and often muscles
were deeply lacerated. It was not uncommon for
the scourge-wounds to penetrate deep into the kid-
neys or lacerate arteries, causing injuries that in

themselves proved fatal. Some victims died from extreme shock during the flogging.

In addition to the physical pain of crucifixion, the most notable feature of this type of execution was the stigma of disgrace that was attached to it. One indignity was the humiliation of carrying one's own cross, which might weigh as much as two hundred pounds. Victims were also mercilessly taunted. They were usually hanged naked. They were deliberately made a spectacle of shame and reproach.

The Crucifixion

When Jesus arrived at Golgotha, why was He offered something to drink?

The soldiers gave Jesus "sour wine mingled with gall to drink. But when He had tasted it, He would not drink" (Matthew 27:34). Apparently just before they nailed Him to the cross, the soldiers offered Him this bitter drink. "Sour wine" is vinegar. "Gall" is something that tastes bitter. Mark 15:23 says the bitter substance was myrrh, which acts as a mild narcotic. So the soldiers may have offered it for its numbing effect just before they drove the nails through the flesh. When Jesus tasted what it was, He spat it out. He did not want His senses numbed. He had come to the cross to be a sin-bearer, and He would feel the full effect of the sin He bore; He would endure the full measure of its pain. The Father had given Him a cup to drink more bitter than the gall of myrrh, but without the stupefying effect. His heart was still steadfastly set on doing the will of the Father, and He would do exactly that.

Jesus was crucified. What did death by crucifixion actually entail?

Jesus would have been nailed to the cross as it lay flat on the ground. The nails used were long, tapered iron spikes, similar to modern railroad spikes, but much sharper. The nails had to be driven through the wrists (not the palms of the hands), because neither the tendons nor the bone structure in the hands could support the body's weight. Nails in the palms would simply tear the flesh between the bones. Nails through the wrists would usually shatter carpal bones and tear the carpal ligaments, but the structure of the wrist was nonetheless strong enough to support the weight of the body. As the nail went into the wrist, it would usually cause severe damage to the sensorimotor median nerve, causing intense pain in both arms. Finally, a single nail would be driven through both feet, sometimes through the Achilles' tendons. None of the nail wounds would be fatal, but they would all cause intense and increasing pain as the victim's time on the cross dragged on.

After the victim was nailed in place, several soldiers would slowly elevate the top of the cross and carefully slide the foot into a deep posthole. The cross would drop with a jarring blow into the bottom of the hole, causing the full weight of the victim to be immediately borne by the nails in the wrists and feet. That would cause a bone-wrenching pain throughout the body, as major joints were suddenly twisted out of their natural position. That is probably what Christ referred to prophetically in Psalm 22, a psalm about the crucifixion: "I am poured out like water, and all my bones are out of joint" (v. 14 NIV).

Is death by crucifixion often death by asphyxiation?

Lack of oxygen is definitely a key contributor to death on a cross. Truman Davis, a medical doctor who studied the physical effects of crucifixion, described how Jesus would have died from lack of oxygen:

> As the arms fatigue, great waves of cramps sweep over the muscles, knotting them in deep, relentless, throbbing pain. With these cramps comes the inability to push Himself upward. As Jesus hangs by His arms, the pectoral muscles are paralyzed and the intercostal muscles are unable to act. Air can be drawn into the lungs, but cannot be exhaled. Jesus fights to raise Himself in order to get even one short breath. Finally, carbon dioxide builds up in the lungs and in the blood stream and the cramps partially subside. Spasmodically He is able to push Himself upward to exhale and bring in the life-giving oxygen.... Hours of this

limitless pain, cycles of twisting, joint-rending cramps, intermittent partial asphyxiation, searing pain as tissue is torn from His lacerated back as He moves up and down against the rough timber; then another agony begins. A deep crushing pain in the chest as the pericardium slowly fills with serum and begins to compress the heart. It is now almost over—the loss of tissue fluid has reached a critical level—the compressed heart is struggling to pump heavy, thick, sluggish blood into the tissues—the tortured lungs are making a frantic effort to gasp in small gulps of air.[1]

Once strength or feeling in the legs was gone, the victim would be unable to push up in order to breathe, and death would occur quickly. That is why the Romans sometimes practiced *crucifracture*—the breaking of the legs below the knees—when they wanted to hasten the process (John 19:31). Dehydration, hypovolemic shock, and congestive heart failure sometimes hastened death as well. In Jesus' case, it seems likely that acute exhaustion was probably another major contributing factor.

---

1. "The Crucifixion of Jesus: The Passion of Christ from a Medical Point of View," *Arizona Medicine*, vol. 22, no. 3 (March 1965), 183–87.

The Justice
of Calvary

Was Jesus' death at Calvary
the worst miscarriage of
human justice in history?

I t was. It was an evil act, perpetrated by the
hands of wicked men. But that is not the full
story. The crucifixion of Christ was also the greatest act of divine justice ever carried out. It was
done in full accord with "the determined purpose
and foreknowledge of God" (Acts 2:23)—and for the
highest of purposes: the death of Christ secured
the salvation of untold numbers and opened the
way for God to forgive sin without compromising
His own perfectly holy standard.

Christ was no mere victim of unjust men when He hung on the cross. Though murdered unjustly and illegally by men whose intentions were only evil, Christ died willingly, becoming an atonement for the sins of the very ones who killed Him. The cross was the outpouring of divine judgment against the person of Christ—not because *He* deserved that judgment, but because He bore it on behalf of those whom He would redeem. It was the greatest sacrifice ever made; the purest act of love ever carried out; and ultimately an infinitely higher act of divine justice than all the human injustice it represented.

Were the people who crucified Jesus innocent pawns in a divine plan?

The designs of those who killed Christ were entirely murderous, and those individuals are by no means exonerated from their evil just because God's purposes are good. The crucifixion of Jesus was still the act of "lawless hands" (Acts 2:23). It was, as far as the human perpetrators were concerned, the ultimate act of pure evil. The wickedness of the crucifixion is in no sense mitigated by the fact that God sovereignly ordained it for good. The truth that it was His sovereign plan makes the deed itself no less a diabolical act of murder. And yet this *was* clearly God's holy and sovereign plan from before the foundation of the world (Revelation 13:8).

How could a loving God approve of this plan, especially when it involved the death of His only Son?

It does give one pause to realize that God ordained the murder of Jesus. Or, to put it starkly in the terms of Isaiah 53:10, that it *pleased* the Lord to bruise Him. God the Father was pleased by the death of His Son only because He was pleased by the redemption that Jesus' death and resurrection accomplished. God the Father was pleased that His eternal plan of salvation was thus fulfilled. He was pleased with the sacrifice of His Son, who died so that others might have eternal life. He was pleased to display His righteous anger against sin in such a graphic way. He was pleased to demonstrate His love for sinners through this majestic sacrifice.

So the crucifixion of Jesus— the death of the Son—was part of God's plan?

The evil plot to kill an innocent man would ultimately succeed, but only in accord with God's plan and only according to His divine timetable. In fact, had the murder of Jesus not been part of the eternal plan of God, it would never have happened. Jesus said of His life, "No one takes it from Me, but I lay it down of Myself. I have power to lay it down, and I have power to take it again. This command I have received from My Father" (John 10:18). Pilate would attempt to force Jesus to answer the accusations against Him by citing his own authority as governor—"Do You not know that I have power to crucify You, and power to release You?" (John 19:10). But Jesus replied, "You could have no power at all against Me unless it had been given you from above" (v. 11). Clearly, God was utterly sovereign in every aspect of what was occurring. The plot devised against Jesus by His enemies was in perfect accord with the plan of God from eternity past.

What did the crucifixion mean for Jesus as a flesh-and-blood human being?

It was no hyperbole when Jesus told the disciples in the garden of Gethsemane that His distress was so severe that it had brought Him to the very brink of death. The agony He bore in the garden was literally sufficient to kill Him—and may well have done so if God were not preserving Him for another means of death. Luke records that "His sweat became like great drops of blood falling down to the ground" (Luke 22:44). That describes a rare but well-documented malady known as *hematidrosis* that sometimes occurs under heavy emotional distress. Subcutaneous capillaries burst under stress and the blood mingles with one's perspiration, exiting through the sweat glands. And the physical agony would become unspeakably worse.

Jesus' Final Words

Scripture records only seven brief sayings from the Savior as He hung on the cross. What is the significance of each of those?

A Plea for Forgiveness

"Father, forgive them, for they do not know what they do." (Luke 23:34)

Jesus' first words from the cross were a plea for mercy on behalf of His tormentors. J. C. Ryle wrote, "As soon as the blood of the Great Sacrifice began to flow, the Great High Priest began to intercede."[1] Christ responded in precisely the

---

1. J. C. Ryle, *Expository Thoughts on the Gospels: Luke Volume 2* (New York: Robert Carter, 1879), 467.

opposite way most men would have. Instead of threatening, lashing back, or cursing His enemies, He prayed to God on their behalf. Even at the very height of His agony, compassion filled His heart. Yet the phrase "for they do not know what they do" does not suggest that they were unaware that they were sinning. Most were fully aware of the *fact* of their wrongdoing, but they were ignorant of the *enormity* of their crime. They were blinded to the full reality that they were crucifying God the Son.

A Promise of Salvation

"Assuredly, I say to you, today you will be with Me in Paradise." (Luke 23:43)

Christ's second utterance shows how generously forgiveness is bestowed. The thief being crucified next to Jesus confessed his own guilt, acknowledged the justice of his own death penalty, and affirmed the innocence of Christ. Yet Jesus promised him paradise. This incident is one of the greatest biblical illustrations of the truth of justification by faith. This man had done nothing to merit salvation, and hanging from a cross, he had no hope of ever earning Christ's favor. He wasn't expected to atone for his own sins, do penance, or perform any ritual. Instead, his forgiveness was full, free, and immediate.

A Provision for His Mother

Although He was dying under the most excruciating kind of anguish, Jesus selflessly provided for His mother (John 19:26–27). Christ loved and honored His mother *as a mother*. He fulfilled the fifth commandment as perfectly as He fulfilled them all. And part of the responsibility of honoring one's parents is the duty to see that they are cared for in their old age. Christ did not neglect that duty.

A Petition to the Father

> "Eli, Eli, lama sabachthani?" that is, "My God, My God, why have You forsaken Me?" (Matthew 27:46)

As Christ hung there, He was bearing the sins of the world, and God was punishing His own Son as if He had committed every wicked deed done by every sinner who would ever believe. And God did it so that He could forgive and treat those redeemed ones as if they had lived Christ's perfect life of righteousness (2 Corinthians 5:21). It was God's own wrath against sin, God's own righteousness, and God's own sense of justice that Christ satisfied on the cross. The physical pains of crucifixion—dreadful as they were—were nothing compared to the wrath of the Father against Him. In that awful, sacred hour, it was as if the Father abandoned Him. Though there was surely no interruption in the Father's love for Him *as a Son,* God nonetheless turned away from Him and forsook Him *as our Substitute.*

A Pleading for Relief

"I thirst!" (John 19:28)

As the end neared, Christ uttered a final plea for physical relief. Earlier He had spat out the vinegar mixed with painkiller that had been offered Him. Now, when He asked for relief from the horrible thirst of dehydration, He was given only a sponge saturated with pure vinegar (John 19:29 NIV). In His thirst we see the true humanity of Christ. Although He was God incarnate, in His physical body, He suffered to an extent few have ever suffered.

A Proclamation of Victory

"It is finished!" (John 19:30) was a cry of triumph. The work the Father had given Jesus to do was now complete. Christ's atoning work was finished; redemption for sinners was complete; and He had conquered sin and death. Christ had fulfilled on behalf of sinners everything the law of God required of them. Full atonement had been made. Everything the ceremonial law foreshadowed had been accomplished. God's justice was satisfied. The ransom for sin was paid in full. The wages of sin were settled forever. All that remained was for Christ to die so that He might rise again.

A Prayer of Consummation

"Father, into Your hands I commit My spirit" expressed the unqualified submission that had been in Jesus' heart from the very beginning (Luke 23:46). In one sense Christ was murdered by the hands of wicked men (Acts 2:23). In another sense it was the Father who sent Him to the cross—and it pleased the Father to do so (Isaiah 53:10). Yet in still another sense, no one took Christ's life: He gave it up willingly for those whom He loved (John 10:17–18). When He finally expired on the cross, it was not with a wrenching struggle against His killers. He did not display any frenzied death throes. His final passage into death—like every other aspect of the crucifixion drama—was a deliberate act of His own sovereign will. John says, "Bowing His head, He gave up His spirit" (John 19:30). Quietly, submissively, He simply yielded up his life.

Jesus: Why He Matters

Christ was dead, but death had not conquered Him. On the first day of the week, He burst forth triumphantly from the grave and showed Himself alive to hundreds of eyewitnesses (1 Corinthians 15:5–8). He not only atoned for sin, but He demonstrated His mastery over death in the process.

The Death of Jesus

Why did the apostle Paul place so much emphasis on the death of Christ rather than always stressing the triumph of the resurrection?

Paul emphasized Christ's death because without the atoning work Christ did on the cross, His resurrection would be merely a wonder to stand back and admire. But it would have no personal ramifications for us. Because of the death Jesus died, suffering the penalty of sin on our behalf, we become partakers with Him in His resurrection as well. That is why "Jesus Christ and him crucified" (1 Corinthians 2:2 NIV) remains the very heart and soul of the gospel message.

Jesus died on Friday, but He rose on Sunday. How is that three days?

When Jews referred to dates and times, they included any portion of a day as a day. Christ had been crucified on Friday and died before sunset (day 1). He had remained buried all day Saturday (day 2). And the women arrived at the tomb on Sunday morning. So when calculating the number of days that had passed since Jesus died, this Sunday was the third day.

What were some of the remarkable, supernatural phenomena that accompanied Jesus' death—and what was the significance of each?

- At noon *darkness* fell over the land and remained for three hours (Matthew 27:45). It could not have been an eclipse, because Passover always fell on a full moon, and a solar eclipse would be out of the question during a full moon. God is certainly able to dim the sun's light. Scripture does not say why the darkness occured; it only reports it as a fact. It may well signify the Father's judgment falling on Christ as He bore in His person our guilt.

- At the moment of Christ's death, "the *veil* of the temple was *torn in two* from top to bottom" (Matthew 27:51). The veil was a heavy curtain that blocked the entrance to the Most Holy Place in the Jerusalem temple, the place where the ark of the covenant was kept, symbolizing the sacred presence of God. The tearing of the curtain at the moment of Jesus' death dramatically symbolized that His sacrifice was a sufficient atonement for sins forever and that the way into Most Holy Place was now open. The tearing of the high curtain from top to bottom signified that it was God Himself who removed the barrier.

• Also at the exact moment of Christ's death, "the *earth quaked*, and the rocks were split" (Matthew 27:51). Although earthquakes were a fairly common phenomenon, an earthquake with enough force to split rocks would have instantly brought the entire city of Jerusalem to a halt for several minutes. A supernatural earthquake like this one could only signify the wrath of God. At the cross, the wrath of God against sin was poured out on His own Son; the accompanying earthquake was a kind of divine punctuation mark.

- At the very same moment when Christ died, "the *graves were opened*; and many bodies of the saints who had fallen asleep were raised" (Matthew 27:52). Their appearance proved that Christ had conquered death, not merely for Himself, but for all believers.
- Mark reports the *conversion of the centurion* charged with overseeing the crucifixion. At the moment of Jesus' death, as Christ's atoning work was brought to completion, its dramatic saving power was already at work in the lives of those who were physically closest to Him. The centurion proclaimed, "Truly this Man was the Son of God!" (Mark 15:39).

Why did Jesus die?

Jesus went to the cross willingly, knowingly, and in submissive obedience to God—to die for others' sins. He endured that shame, that disgrace, that pain, and the wrath of God against the sin He bore, for the joy set before Him—the redemption of His people.

On the cross God was punishing His own Son as if He had committed every wicked deed done by every sinner who would ever believe. And He did it so that He could forgive and treat those redeemed ones as if they had lived Christ's perfect life of righteousness. It was God's own wrath against sin, God's own righteousness, and God's own sense of justice that Christ satisfied on the cross. Christ died in our place and in our stead—and He received the outpouring of divine wrath in all its fury that we deserved for our sin. It was a punishment so severe that a mortal man could spend all eternity in the torments of hell, and still he would not have begun to exhaust the divine wrath that was heaped on Christ at the cross.

The Resurrection

How can we be sure that Jesus actually rose from the dead?

Christ's resurrection is one of the central truths of the Christian faith and the only plausible explanation for the empty tomb. Even the Jewish leaders did not deny the reality of the empty tomb but concocted the story that the disciples had stolen Jesus' body (Matthew 28:11–15). The idea that the fearful (John 20:19), doubting (John 20:24–25) disciples somehow overpowered the Roman guard detachment and stole Jesus' body is absurd. That they did it while the guards were asleep is even more preposterous. Surely, in moving the heavy stone from the mouth of the tomb, the disciples would have awakened at least one of the soldiers.

And in any case, how could the guards have known what happened while they were asleep? Many other theories have been invented over the centuries to explain away the empty tomb, all of them equally futile.

Who saw the resurrected Jesus?

Mary Magdalene was the first to see the risen Jesus, even mistaking Him for the gardener (John 20:14–16). Jesus next greeted the women who were on their way to Jerusalem to tell the disciples that the tomb was empty (Matthew 28:9). Then, although Jesus had told His disciples, "After I have been raised, I will go before you to Galilee" (Matthew 26:32), Jesus did not appear to the disciples first in Galilee. He actually came to them on several occasions before meeting them there. He appeared first to Peter (Luke 24:34). He met two disciples on the road to Emmaus (Luke 24:13–15). On the evening of Resurrection Sunday, He met the ten disciples who were assembled (John 20:19), and eight days later all eleven, after Thomas had joined them (John 20:26). But Jesus' supreme appearance was set to take place in Galilee. There "He was seen by over five hundred brethren at once" (1 Corinthians 15:6), and it was there that the eleven disciples were commissioned to their apostolic ministry.

Why has the resurrection of Jesus Christ been called the single greatest event in the history of the world?

The resurrection of Jesus from the dead is so foundational to Christianity that no one who denies it can be a true Christian. Without resurrection there is no Christian faith, no salvation, and no hope. "If there is no resurrection of the dead," Paul explained, "then Christ is not risen. And if Christ is not risen, then our preaching is empty and your faith is also empty" (1 Corinthians 15:13–14). A person who believes in a Christ who was not raised believes in a powerless Christ, a dead Christ. If Christ did not rise from the dead, then no redemption was accomplished at the cross. "Your faith is futile; you are still in your sins!" (1 Corinthians 15:17).

It is hardly surprising, therefore, that the first sermon on the day the church was born focused on the resurrection of Christ. After charging his hearers with Jesus' death, Peter declared, "Whom God raised up, having loosed the pains of death, because it was not possible that He should be held by it" (Acts 2:24). The resurrection stands as a central theme in Paul's epistles as well. He declared that Christ "was buried, and that He rose again the third day according to the Scriptures" (1 Corinthians 15:4). Salvation belongs only to those who believe in the resurrection of Jesus Christ, who confess Him as Lord and Savior, and who thereby identify themselves with Him.

The Choice
Between Life
and Death

Why does it matter who Jesus is?

For the same reason it matters what we think about God. And your view of God automatically has more far-reaching ramifications than anything else in your belief system. What you think of God will automatically color how you think about everything else—especially how you prioritize values; how you determine right and wrong; and what you think of your own place in the universe. That in turn will surely determine how you act.

Someone who rejects God has repudiated the

only reasonable foundation for morality, account-ability, true spirituality, and the necessary distinction between good and evil. So the atheist's private life will inevitably become a living demonstration of the evils of unbelief. To whatever degree some atheists seek to maintain a public veneer of virtue and respectability—as well as when they themselves make moral judgments about others—they are walking contradictions. What possible "virtue" could there be in an accidental universe with no Lawgiver and no Judge?

What are the possible consequences of what we believe about God?

One of the central themes of the Bible is the importance of believing the truth about God. This is not something the Bible merely hints at or lightly glosses over. Statement after statement in Scripture emphatically declare that our view of God is the most fundamental spiritual issue of all. In biblical terms, the difference between true faith and false belief (or unbelief) is the difference between life and death, heaven and hell.

What are some guidelines for considering who God is?

Two nonnegotiable theological convictions that we are wise to bring to this discussion are, first, a commitment to the absolute accuracy and authority of Scripture—as the revealed Word of God, not as a product of human imagination, experience, intuition, or ingenuity (2 Peter 1:21). The other is a strong belief that the gospel sets forth the only possible way of salvation from sin and judgment—by grace through faith in the Lord Jesus Christ.

Let's face it: the idea that the entire human race is fallen and condemned is simply too harsh for most people's tastes. They would rather believe that most people are fundamentally good. All we need to do, they say, is cultivate our underlying goodness, and we can fix everything wrong with human society. (That's not terribly different from what the Pharisees believed about themselves.) But Scripture says otherwise. We are hopelessly corrupted by sin. All who do not have Christ as Lord and Savior are in bondage to evil, condemned by a just God, and bound for hell.

Twenty-first-century people try hard not to offend individuals who have different beliefs; tolerance and acceptance are the rule of the day. That doesn't seem to be the choice Jesus made, however. What can we learn from Him?

Sometimes—especially when a vitally important biblical truth is under assault; when the souls of people are at stake; or (above all) when the gospel message is being mangled by false teachers—sometimes it is simply wrong to let a contrary opinion be aired without any challenge or correction. One of the worst things a believer can do is show a kind of feigned academic respect or artificial cordiality to the purveyors of serious, soul-destroying error (Psalm 129:4–8; 1 Corinthians 16:22). The notion that an amiable conversation is always superior to open conflict is quite contrary to the example Christ Himself has given us.

Jesus as Savior and Lord

What is the connection between naming Jesus "Lord" and acknowledging Him as Savior?

Jesus is Lord, and those who refuse Him as Lord cannot use Him as Savior. Everyone who receives Him (Savior) must surrender to His authority (Lord), for to say we receive Christ when in fact we reject His right to reign over us is utter absurdity. It is a futile attempt to hold on to sin with one hand and take Jesus with the other. What kind of salvation is it if we are left in bondage to sin?

This, then, is the gospel we are to proclaim: That Jesus Christ, who is God incarnate, humbled

Himself to die on our behalf. Thus He became the sinless sacrifice to pay the penalty of our guilt. He rose from the dead to declare with power that He is Lord over all, and He offers eternal life freely to sinners who will surrender to Him in humble, repentant faith. This gospel promises nothing to the haughty rebel, but for broken, penitent sinners, it graciously offers everything that pertains to life and godliness (2 Peter 1:3).

To give glory to Christ, we must confess Him as Lord. That's a part of salvation, not a subsequent act. Salvation is a matter of confessing that Christ is God and, therefore, that He is sovereign in your life.

What does having faith in Jesus as one's Savior look like in real life?

Scripture describes faith as a wholehearted trust in Christ personally (Galatians 2:16; Philippians 3:9). Not merely faith *about* Him; faith *in* Him. Note the difference: If I say I believe some promise you have made, I am saying far less than if I say I trust *you*. Believing in a person necessarily involves some degree of commitment. Trusting Christ means placing oneself in His custody for both life and death. It means we rely on His counsel, trust in His goodness, and entrust ourselves for time and eternity to His guardianship. Real faith, saving faith, is all of me (mind, emotions, and will) embracing all of Him (Savior, Advocate, Provider, Sustainer, Counselor, and Lord God).

Those who have such faith will love Christ (John 8:42; 14:15; Romans 8:28). They will therefore want to do His bidding. How could someone who truly believes in Christ continue to defy His authority and pursue what He hates? In this sense, then, the crucial issue for lordship salvation is not merely authority and submission, but the affections of the heart. Jesus as Lord is far more than just an authority figure. He's also our highest treasure and most precious companion. We obey Him out of sheer delight.

So the gospel demands surrender, not only for authority's sake, but also because surrender is the believer's highest joy. Such surrender is not an extraneous adjunct to faith; it is the very essence of believing.

Turning to Jesus

Repentant faith is the requirement. It is not merely a decision to trust Christ for eternal life, but a wholesale forsaking of everything else we trust, and a turning to Jesus Christ as Lord and Savior.

- **Repent**: "Repent, and turn away from all your transgressions" (Ezekiel 18:30). "'I have no pleasure in the death of anyone who dies,' declares the Lord God. 'Therefore, repent and live'" (Ezekiel 18:32 NASB). "God is now declaring to men that all everywhere should repent" (Acts 17:30 NASB). "Repent and turn to God, performing deeds appropriate to repentance" (Acts 26:20 NASB).
- **Turn your heart** *from all that you know dishonors God*: "[Turn] to God from idols to serve a living and true God" (1 Thessalonians 1:9).

- **Trust Him** *as Lord and Savior*: "Believe in the Lord Jesus, and you will be saved" (Acts 16:31 NASB). "If you confess with your mouth Jesus as Lord, and believe in your heart that God raised Him from the dead, you will be saved" (Romans 10:9 NASB).
- **Follow Jesus**: "If anyone wishes to come after Me, let him deny himself, and take up his cross daily and follow Me" (Luke 9:23 NASB). "No one, after putting his hand to the plow and looking back, is fit for the kingdom of God" (Luke 9:62 NASB). "If anyone serves Me, let him follow Me; and where I am, there shall My servant also be; if anyone serves Me, him My Father will honor" (John 12:26).

Jesus' Invitation to You

To embrace Jesus in saving faith and enter His eternal kingdom, you must first acknowledge your sinfulness before God. Like the tax collector in Luke 18:13–14, you must ask God for mercy and forgiveness, trusting not in your own good works but only in the finished work of His Son, Jesus Christ. Through His death on the cross, Jesus paid the penalty for sin—so that all who believe in Him will be saved. Through His resurrection, Jesus conquered death once and for all and proved that He is who He claimed to be.

True belief is more than just mental assent. Embracing Jesus Christ as your Lord and Savior includes being willing to follow and serve Him. For those who love the Lord Jesus Christ, serving Him is not a burden. Rather it is a profound delight, the fruit of a transformed life, and a preview of the glorious worship that awaits all believers in heaven.

If you confess with your mouth the Lord Jesus and believe in your heart that God has raised Him from the dead, you will be saved. For with the heart one believes unto righteousness, and with the mouth confession is made unto salvation.

—ROMANS 10:9–10

Sources

MacArthur, John F. *Experiencing the Passion of Christ: God's Purpose Behind Christ's Pain*. Nashville, TN: Thomas Nelson, 2004.

———. *God in the Manger: The Miraculous Birth of Christ*. Nashville, TN: Thomas Nelson, 2001.

———. *The Gospel According to the Apostles: The Role of Works in the Life of Faith*. Nashville, TN: Thomas Nelson, 1993 and 2000.

———. *The Jesus You Can't Ignore: What You Must Learn from the Bold Confrontations of Christ*. Nashville, TN: Thomas Nelson, 2008.

———. *The MacArthur Bible Commentary*. Nashville, TN: Thomas Nelson, 2005.

———. *The Murder of Jesus: A Study of How Jesus Died*. Nashville, TN: Thomas Nelson, 2000 and 2004.

———. *The Truth About the Lordship of Christ*. Nashville, TN: Thomas Nelson, 2012.